C000131996

Lindsay Knight has specialised as a writer and programme maker in health and social issues. She worked on a range of magazines, including *New Internationalist* and *New Society*; she edited MIND's monthly magazine, *Mind Out*, and wrote for the *Guardian*, *Cosmopolitan*, *The Sunday Times* and various medical and social services magazines.

She has produced and directed a range of television programmes, including Channel 4's health series 'Well Being' and 'The Pulse'; a 'Dispatches' on psychiatric drugs, and two programmes on mid-life crisis.

Lindsay Knight's first book *Talking to a Stranger* is a guide to psychotherapy and other talking treatments. It was MIND Book of the Year and won the Medical Journalists' Award. In his Foreword to the second edition, Dr Robin Skynner wrote: 'Clear, understandable and enjoyable . . . the reader seeking an overview of this fascinating field could not have a better guide.'

Also by Lindsay Knight

Talking to a Stranger

Why Feeling Bad is Good

Lindsay Knight

Hodder & Stoughton

Copyright © 1996 by Lindsay Knight

First published in Great Britain in 1996 by
Hodder & Stoughton
A division of Hodder Headline PLC

The right of Lindsay Knight to be identified as the Author
of the Work has been asserted by her in accordance with
the Copyright, Designs and Patents Act 1988.

10 9 8 7 6 5 4 3 2 1

All rights reserved. No part of this publication may be
reproduced, stored in a retrieval system, or transmitted
in any form or by any means without the prior written
permission of the publisher, nor be otherwise circulated in
any form of binding or cover other than that in which it
is published and without a similar condition being imposed
on the subsequent purchaser.

A CIP catalogue record for this title is available
from the British Library

ISBN 0 340 62594 5

Typeset by Palimpsest Book Production Limited,
Polmont, Stirlingshire
Printed and bound in Great Britain by
Cox and Wyman Ltd, Reading, Berkshire

Hodder and Stoughton
A division of Hodder Headline PLC
338 Euston Road
London NW1 3BH

Acknowledgements

There are many people who have helped me over the years to learn about the issues described in this book, and to form some of my views. I particularly want to thank the many women who gave so generously of their time, their insights and their often painful memories; their case-histories form the backbone of the book. Several experts have helped me enormously, though any mistakes are mine. I especially want to thank psychotherapists Jill Curtis and Mike Harari, and the late and much missed Britta Harding.

I want to thank Colette Casey and Catherine Townsend for their research work. They are enthusiastic and diligent workers. I want to thank my family – my mother Dorothy Knight, my brother Andrew and his family Jane, Timothy and William – and my many friends for their support and encouragement. I particularly want to thank Sue Davidson, Jill Rowlands, Chris Schwarz and Ros Townsend for their constant and warm friendship and support, not only whilst I was writing this book; Shelley Saywell and Hazel Smyth, who in their delightful ways badgered and boosted me to get this written; and Julian Oliver, for so much. This book is dedicated to him.

Contents

What have we achieved? • Where are the jobs? • Poverty
• Health problems • Violence against women • An
equal society is a healthy society • The world of work •
Unemployment

Fears and anger • The 'bad boy' • Myth and reality
• Losing your 'self': Janet's story • The search
for someone special • Do we depend too much on
relationships?: addicted to love; Anna's story; Christine's
story • Men who exploit our 'weaknesses': Kate's story
• Is it different for younger women? • Poor marriages:
'I'm drowning': Gina's story • Knowing when it's time
to leave: fears of loneliness imprison us; the value of
friendship • Trying to correct the balance • Enjoying
being single • Ageing with optimism

The tyranny of thinness • What women say • Eating
disorders: the causes; the reality; the treatment • Ageing
• Mid-life crisis? The menopause: challenging our fears •
Combating negative body image

So you're feeling bad • Examining the present •
Examining the past • Facing up to reality • So you're
feeling bad – that can be good • Think positive! •
Celebrate friendships • Be kind to your body: eat well;
avoid alcohol; learn to enjoy exercise; learn to relax •
Talking treatments: finding the right therapist • Drugs •
Stepping out

Introduction

The facts of the matter

The statistics are horrifying. Rates of depression are at least twice as high among women as among men in the UK, United States and most of the western world. At any one point in time, at least one fifth of women aged sixteen and over in the UK will be suffering some depressive symptoms. That is almost five million women.

Women are far more likely than men to be diagnosed by their doctors as suffering from psychological problems. Throughout Europe and North America, we are prescribed at least twice as many psychotropic, or mind-altering drugs (tranquillisers, sedatives, anti-depressants) as men. One study, reported in *Promoting Women's Health* by Rachel Jenkins, found that twice as many women as men received ten or more prescriptions for psychotropic drugs in a year.[1] Another report, quoted in MIND's publication *Eve Fights Back*, states that two thirds of people in the UK taking anti-depressants are women.[2] Depression is still treated by ECT (electric shock treatment), which is a very controversial treatment, and various studies indicate that the majority of patients given ECT – around seventy per cent – are women.

These are the official figures from family doctors and various reports, based on descriptions of clinically recognisable patterns of psychological symptoms. So these are figures based on those people diagnosed as suffering from depression, and then given some form of treatment. But it is estimated that doctors do not detect about forty per cent of mental illness in the community. Many of these people will be depressed, and many will be women who do not realise they are depressed. When we go to the doctor, we are more likely to talk about feeling tired 'all the time' or having bad headaches. We may 'just feel low' most days, but see this as part of our lot, something to put up with, not to make a fuss about. Many of us who are depressed lead lives of 'quiet desperation'. We may not even consider talking to our family doctor. We may suspect something is wrong, we may drink a little too much or smoke heavily, but then just accept this is part of life's normal pattern. These feelings may be linked to a poor marriage or the aftermath of a divorce.

In *Social Focus on Women*, published in 1995, a fifth of women aged between sixteen and sixty-four were found to have suffered 'some form of neurotic disorder' the week before they were interviewed. The four most common symptoms were fatigue, sleep problems, irritability and worry – four very common symptoms of depression.[3]

For some of us, the depression may become so crippling that we are offered specialist psychiatric help, perhaps admission to a psychiatric hospital or unit. Once again, women are over represented statistically among psychiatric patients compared with men. But for the majority of us who are depressed, medical support will consist of a pack of pills, or nothing at all.

Psychotherapist Jill Curtis describes this problem as: 'A river of women meandering along with low-grade depression. Most will never consider counselling or therapy. They don't want to make a fuss.' But depression damages the quality of our lives, our relationships, perhaps our work, and our potential for change and growth. Depression stunts us as women, it deprives us of emotional nourishment from ourselves and, usually, from others. How many of us recognise the following descriptions?

'It felt like being at the bottom of a black hole.'

'The birds didn't sing in my garden any more.'

We are confronting a major problem. Too many of us just aren't healthy enough mentally, and some of us don't even acknowledge that we don't have to live like this. And if we decide we want to change, what help is available? What can we do?

Are men any healthier mentally? Not necessarily, but they display mental dis-ease in other ways. They drink too much, or become violent. They may suppress their feelings and become physically ill. They are far more reluctant to admit to psychological problems, either to their doctor or those close to them. Thus, more men than women 'succeed' in killing themselves (over three times as many suicides are men) though more women attempt suicide. And it would seem that doctors are less likely to diagnose men's symptoms as psychological, as compared with doctors' attitudes towards women's problems. Nor, as I'll explain later in the book, do men confront the same social or psycho-social problems as women. We may have moved a long way in the past thirty or so years, but we still live with attitudes and practices which discriminate against women, and make our lives deeply stressful.

What surprises, and upsets, me as I've researched this book, is the discovery that the reasons for depression are often the same at whatever age. Younger women may seem more confident, and obviously have benefitted from the achievements of the women's movement. But they often report being depressed for the very same reasons as their mothers in their forties and fifties:

'I wish I was thinner, I hate the way I look.'

'I'd be much happier if I had a boyfriend, it always makes me feel more socially acceptable.'

A Health Education Authority report on thirteen-and fourteen-year-olds, published in 1995, showed that teenage girls suffer much lower self-esteem than their male counterparts – despite the fact that most of the girls are more successful academically.[4] Low self-esteem and depression walk hand in hand. So who says we can put feminism behind us?

Feeling bad can be good

My aim in this book is to explore the various causes of women's depression, and then to show that depression is often a very normal reaction to what is happening in a woman's life. It can be a very healthy response to a very *un*healthy situation.

But however healthy a response, what's positive about depression? How can feeling bad be good for us? Because, I believe, we must accept that the emotional pain we call depression, in its myriad and miserable manifestations, is a message, a signal. It is telling us something is wrong in our world. And I don't mean wrong in, for example, the obvious way that we don't have a man around at the moment. It should be, and is, possible to be your own woman without a partner around all the time. You may feel sad at times, frustrated, lonely, but you won't be constantly depressed.

No, depression is telling us something is more seriously amiss in our psyche. Feelings of depression, or those psychosomatic conditions linked with depression, such as anorexia and other eating disorders, make clear the link between our inner and outer worlds, and show how the two interact and influence each other. If we are depressed, apparently because we don't have a boyfriend or because we feel fat, we have to make sense of that feeling, to discover the real, underlying cause, so that we can deal with it and, I believe, move on to a healthier and happier way of living. Through self-exploration, perhaps with the aid of a therapist or counsellor, we can work out the patterns we destructively repeat in our lives, and the inappropriate responses we may have to certain situations and emotions.

Exploring the causes

In this book, I shall explore the various reasons why women become depressed rather than angry, why we sit in a heap rather than going out and attacking the weeds or being active in some other way. We waste so much energy in being depressed, energy which could be put to so much use for our delight, our benefit. I shall explore the reasons why loss of a partner or work, or anticipating that loss, causes such turmoil. I have talked to experts and, above all, to a range of women from their late teens to their sixties and seventies. I explore various triggers for depression, such as relationship problems, or lack of work, status etc., and ask what makes so many of us so vulnerable to depression.

I am not writing this from a wholly objective, or from a 'holier than thou' standpoint. When I wrote my first book, a guide to psychotherapy and other talking treatments, I believed at first I could research it without experiencing therapy for myself. Little did I realise that I had almost certainly wanted to write such a book in order to 'give myself permission' to undertake therapy – which I inevitably did soon after I began the research. I have consequently concluded that by and large we choose the path we take and we make our own 'luck'. Perhaps nothing is an accident.

Thus it is no accident that I have been commissioned to write a book about depression, and with a particular slant – the idea of 'healthy' depression. I'm a woman, I do experience depression from time to time, and I do believe that we should 'listen to' our depression, that, as one woman said to me, it's sending us messages, telling us something is wrong in our world, that we should change the way we live. Carl Jung, one of the great founding fathers of psychotherapy, believed that neurotic symptoms such as depression appeared when people felt 'stuck', when their lives seemed to lack meaning and significance. And, he argued, through 'breakdown' we could reach 'breakthrough'.

Not that I'd advocate depression as an easy route to change; it's bloody and painful, and can be fatal. But because depression is so common, because the pain and loss which lead to depression are so common, I believe we must first acknowledge its existence and its power and, secondly, use it to improve our lot, our life. To make a rather simplistic analogy with physical hurt, if you have a bad physical pain you will eventually seek medical advice as pain usually means something is wrong. But often the response to emotional pain has been 'pull yourself together', 'be a man' (even if you're a woman), 'cheer up and have a drink'. But ignoring emotional pains can be as dangerous in the long run as ignoring physical symptoms.

Reaping the benefits

Many of us have spent years of our lives, and huge amounts of money, trying to be physically fit. But, without denying the psychological benefits of exercise, I wonder why we don't work harder to become healthier mentally? Why do so many of us put up with a disabling condition – depression – in a way that we would never accept a physical disability? Partly, I am sure, because to admit to any form of emotional problem is often seen as a sign of weakness. So we deny, consciously or unconsciously, that we are depressed. We blame tiredness, the weather, a bad day at work. Or we drown our sorrows, or smoke them away. Anything but admit to the black hole in our psyche.

I want to show that by exploring that black hole, we can become healthier mentally. That doesn't mean deliriously happy all of the time but it does mean, put simply, the ability to cope with life, the highs and the lows, and the dreary inbetweens. It should mean the ability to cope with change, to welcome it even, to be flexible in mind and spirit. It doesn't necessarily exile depression forever from our lives, but by understanding why we feel low, we should deal with it more positively, turning it into anger and action. Such an exploration is neither easy nor painless, but, to quote Plato: 'The unexamined life is not worth living.'

How to use the book

You may find it helpful to read through the book once to grasp my ideas and thoughts, then to read it again more slowly and reflect on how my approach to depression fits in with your experience.

I have listed Learning Points at the end of each chapter, and the final chapter, plus Resource Guide and Book List should give more practical help too.

There is inevitably some repetition but this is deliberate, to reinforce the message and help readers focus on the important ideas.

1   What Depression Feels Like

> She left the room undusted, did not care
> To hang a picture, even lay a book
> On the small table. All her pain was there—
> In absences. The furious window shook
> With violent storms she had no power to share.
>
> Her face was lined, her bones stood thinly out
> She spoke, it's true, but not as if it mattered;
> She helped with washing-up and things like that.
> Her face looked anguished when the china clattered.
> Mostly she merely stared at us and sat . . .
>
> Elizabeth Jennings, *A Depression*

We all think we know what it is like to be depressed –
unhappy, fed up because *he* hasn't called or we haven't
enough money for a decent holiday. Indeed, the term
depression does cover a wide range of moods, from everyday
'fed upness' to the bleakness of feeling that life is a prison, a
black hole, and suicide seems the only way out.

This book is not for those lucky women who are fed up
from time to time but, on the whole, fairly contented with
their lot. It is for those of us – and there are many – whose
experience of depression is more regular, ranging across the
spectrum from grey to black. Our responses to depression
too will vary from one woman to another.

Anne is a thirty-year-old surveyor who becomes depressed

whenever there is a major upset in her life. Anne understands that depression is her response to job insecurity, or a relationship break-up. She is beginning therapy to understand what it is in her psychological make-up that makes her react in such a way. She wants to break the pattern.

Jane doesn't often admit she is depressed. Divorced after ten years of marriage, caring for two small children, she finds life hard as a single mother, trying to forge a new career after years at home. She is actually very angry: angry with her faithless ex-husband, angry with her parents who also divorced, angry with herself for being a 'failure'. But she doesn't acknowledge this anger to herself because confrontation, strong feelings, terrify her. Instead, she drinks, often a bottle of wine or more a night. If a friend is round, she may become quite hysterical. But the next day she often doesn't remember what she said and may be quite cool to her friend. When another friend gently suggested therapy might help her, she dismissed the idea completely.

Although every woman's experience of depression is unique, the emotions expressed and the symptoms reported are often very similar:

'I feel worthless and ashamed. I hate the way I look, the way I am.'

'It is like being at the bottom of a black pit or a black hole.'

'Life is bleak, with nothing to look forward to.'

'I feel immobilised, unable to function well.'

'I drink too much, smoke too much.'

'I eat too much – or, on the other hand, I can hardly bear to eat, it makes me feel sick.'

'I feel I don't really exist. I lead my life, go to work, look after my family, but I often feel transparent.'

'I can lie in bed most of the day. There I feel secure, bed is wonderful.'

'I wanted a bus to mount the pavement and run me over. I didn't have the energy to manage death on my own.'

If you find yourself agreeing with one or more of these statements, this book can help you. But in order to understand and learn from our experience of depression, we must first look in more detail at the symptoms and what causes it.

The symptoms of depression

How can we define depression? The dictionary describes it as a 'State of extreme dejection', a lowering of the spirits. It is a condition or experience which often overwhelms; it can strike suddenly, throwing you into utter despair, or it can hang around for months or years, so that it is like living in a damp cloud on a hilltop.

It is also a defined mental illness, in fact one of the most common. A group of psychiatrists writing in the *British Medical Journal* in 1992 put forward a 'consensus statement' on recognising people with depression, for family doctors.[1] They wrote: 'The term depression describes a continuum of phenomena from a normal mood which is common and affects almost everyone from time to time to a severe disorder. A central feature of all depressive conditions is the lowering of mood, which when more severe may be accompanied by tearfulness and lack of ability to take interest in or pleasure from one's usual activities.' (Medically written material so often lacks the flesh-and-blood misery of the condition.) They continue to explain that: 'As depressions become more pronounced and pathological to reach the level of a psychiatric disorder the disturbance becomes more pervasive and a range of other symptoms develop. In almost all cases there is a characteristic way of thinking, with persistent negative views, which may include thoughts of personal worthlessness and incapacity, guilt about past actions, and pessimism about the future. Ideas of being better off dead develop and thoughts of suicide . . . Disturbances of sleep and appetite are common, usually in the form of a reduction, sometimes of an increase. Other physical symptoms include diurnal variations of mood, loss of energy, slowing of movement and speech, and fears or beliefs of bodily illness. There is impaired concentration, impaired ability to function in work and in a range of other roles, and impaired personal relationships.'

In a later part of the paper, the authors ask why doctors often miss depression in patients. One reason, they argue and I would agree, is that there is still a stigma attached to mental illness. It means many people are reluctant to admit to being depressed, either to themselves or others, and therefore do not seek help.

Although many of us wouldn't risk admitting to depression, we don't mind complaining of backache or migraine, health problems which are often stress-related, but are seen as perfectly valid. Depression is viewed by some as a sign of weakness, of poor moral fibre or lack of backbone, of being unable to cope, of failure, in a way that more obviously physical illness is not. Yet look hard for the causes of feeling low, and that depression may be a perfectly healthy response to emotional or psychological pain – just as a broken leg would ache and tell us a bone needs to be mended.

The common symptoms of depression are constant tiredness, insomnia, frequent bouts of tears, loss of motivation.

When we are depressed, we feel negative about everything, and especially ourselves, guilty and worthless. People who are depressed feel trapped in a prison; they long to escape, but can't escape from themselves and their feelings except briefly, perhaps through alcohol. They often stop eating, as if they are physically trying to disappear. They have no energy and take no pleasure in anything.

> Marian is forty-five. She and her husband separated two years ago, and she vividly remembers how desperate she felt. 'It was as if I was trapped, paralysed almost by the misery I felt. I would try to move, to eat something or make a 'phone call. Even if I succeeded and felt a little better, half an hour later the world was black again. I'd subside into the sofa, usually in tears and just chainsmoke. Looking back, I realise all my energy went into being depressed. I often felt suicidal.'

In 1993, the Royal College of Psychiatrists and the Royal College of General Practitioners jointly initiated the Defeat Depression Campaign, aimed at increasing awareness and understanding of depression, so that those of us suffering from it would not be afraid to seek help. They have produced a card for family doctors to help in diagnosing depression, with relevant questions to ask a patient complaining of a 'low mood'. For example: How bad is the mood and how long have you been low? Have you lost interest in things? Have you lost confidence in yourself?

Not, as I noted earlier, that every woman who is depressed seeks medical help. She may have previously found her doctor unsympathetic, advocating the 'stiff upper lip' approach of traditional English stoicism.

> Coline is a bright, attractive eighteen-year-old, about to go to university. For most of her teens, she has been depressed and it would not take many questions for a doctor to discover this. But when she finally plucked up courage to see her family doctor last year, 'he told me to pull myself together and come back next

week. Yet I was sitting there crying my eyes out.' Needless to say, she did not return.

Jane's GP referred her to the practice counsellor when she explained how miserable and tense she was feeling some years ago. Counselling has helped, as have anti-depressants, but she knows she may need more help. 'I really want to stop taking the anti-depressants but I need the doctor's support, to know when is a good time. He did help me initially but I do feel he doesn't really want to know. He's thinking, "just another neurotic woman".'

The effects of depression

Depression may not prevent people working. They develop strategies to conceal their fragile state and help them cope with their daily routine.

Jillian was a journalist, in her late thirties. She worked on a national newspaper and was successful and well liked. But from time to time, usually because yet another romantic relationship had failed, she became badly depressed. She would go to work and pretend she had a headache or something similar to explain why she wasn't her usual lively self. In the evenings she drank and smoked, and ate very little. Her close friends always recognised something was wrong as yet again she dramatically lost weight. She would lie in bed for hours, her escape route, at weekends, and occasionally during the week would call into work to say she was ill.

Like many depressed women, Jillian managed to function well enough most of the time. For others, depression is so disabling that they feel they are falling apart and cannot possibly lead normal lives. At the extreme end of the spectrum, depression can make women feel suicidal. The last published figures on suicide in the UK show that over 1000 women committed suicide. There are no collected national data on attempted suicides but a report on attempted suicides in Oxford in the years 1991 and 1992 shows an increase in the number of women trying to kill themselves. Also, more women made more than one suicide attempt.

'Hidden' depression

For many of us, it may be a long time before we put two and two together and realise that the various 'feelings' of discomfort and discontent we suffer add up to depression. These are often the women doctors fail to diagnose correctly. It has been estimated that every year, twelve million adults who visit their family doctor have some symptoms of mental illness; some eighty per cent are suffering from anxiety and depression.[2] On average, doctors detect six out of ten cases; of these, nine out of ten are treated by the doctor, and one in ten is referred to specialist psychiatric services. Men are more likely to be referred to specialist services. Single women, young women and those over retirement age are particularly unlikely to have their symptoms of mental distress identified by their doctor as being in need of specialist help. The majority of women I interviewed for this book had never seen a psychiatrist, let alone been admitted to a psychiatric unit or hospital.

> Susan, in her twenties, had felt suicidal every day of her life from an early age. She had experienced a miserable childhood, with a domineering mother who told her she didn't love her and wished she hadn't been born. But her depression was only recognised by anyone, including herself, when she asked her doctor for help to overcome a phobia.

Many women feel weary all the time. They have headaches,

or other aches and pains. They often don't want to get up in the morning. Life seems very dull, tedious in its routine. They will go to bed early and pretend to be asleep to avoid having sex with their partner. Children irritate rather than delight. When a machine breaks down, or food burns, it's a major trauma. Everything is out of kilter. You can see the depression sometimes in the way they walk, often stooped, somehow reflecting the view that they are downtrodden. Dull eyes, hair often uncombed, uncared for, gloomy clothes thrown on. It is a statement; I don't care for myself (and perhaps nobody else does either).

At the other extreme are the women who are always bright, always coping, so brittle you think they may break if they smile yet again. Their heart may be in pieces, their marriage splitting up, their redundancy letter on the table, but they will always keep up appearances. I often wonder if such women unzip their faces along with their clothes in the privacy of their bedroom. They certainly won't admit anything is wrong in their world to others, and often not to themselves.

Fear of anger

All these women are suppressing strong emotions about their lives. The emotion is often anger. Homeopath Sohani Gonzalez often sees women with depression: 'It is so often suppressed anger, anger towards the man in their lives, and a lot aimed at parents. They have learned to suppress anger from an early age. As children, many of us have been told "don't get angry", or "you mustn't cry". Young women have suffered from this as much as the older ones.'

Far too many women not only deny their anger but often too they deny the fact that their anger has been 'turned into' depression. They accept their 'lot'. Psychotherapist Jill Curtis told me: 'I often find myself saying to a woman patient, "It sounds to me as if you can't make a fuss about things," and she says, "Of course I can't." I try to help them become more questioning.'

Janet realised after several months of marriage that she was unhappy. Her husband, apparently charming, attractive, intelligent, loving, too often said he found her lacking; she wasn't nice enough to him, she didn't cook well enough, she was overweight. He never hit her but he was emotionally abusive. She was a smart, attractive, successful writer, but at times he turned her into a quivering mouse. She tried very hard to change herself, though inwardly she might seethe because she didn't think she was so bad. She'd occasionally show her anger and he withdrew emotionally, saying how much she was hurting him. So she tried again to be Mrs Perfect, suppressing all the 'bad' feelings. Sometimes it was OK, but often she felt as if she were playing someone else's part in a play which had nothing to do with her. She started to cry a lot (though hiding this from him) and only slept through the night if she took sedatives.

Janet did not realise that it is impossible to suppress strong feelings, to be untrue to one's real nature. As Sigmund Freud wrote in *Five Lectures*: 'When the bed of a stream is divided into two channels, then, if the current in one of them is brought up against an obstacle, the other will at once be overfilled.'[3] Powerful emotions won't stay down for ever; at some point, they will surface as a mental or physical symptom.

It makes me angry to see the way in which women so often suppress their emotions, and how doctors frequently aid them in this by prescribing drugs which have the same effect. Although the so-called minor tranquillisers such as Valium are not prescribed as much as they were in the 1980s and before, these and other psychotropic (mind-altering) drugs are prescribed twice as often for women as for men. As Heather Ashton wrote in the *British Journal of Psychiatry* in 1991: '. . . it is not uncommon to see people (usually women) who have been taking anti-depressants for many years . . .' Nor is this necessarily age-related. She quotes a study of drug-taking habits among students at Newcastle University in 1983–4. Asked if they had ever been prescribed minor tranquillisers, 14.6 per cent and 10.3 per cent of the medical and non-medical female students said Yes, compared with 4.2 per cent and 6.5 per cent of the men respectively. 'Thus, even at the average age of 19 years, women are more likely to go to their general practitioners and be prescribed a tranquilliser than men.'[4]

Ashton explains that all the studies of drug-taking show that *at all ages* women consume twice as many psychotropic drugs as men. She concludes that: '. . . it does appear to be true that doctors are more likely to perceive illness in women as having a psychological rather than a physical basis, and this perception makes them more likely to prescribe psychotropic drugs.'

In June 1993 Princess Diana addressed a conference on drugs, given by the charity Turning Point. She demanded more help for women victims of mental pressure. She explained that: 'Women in our society are seen as the carers, the ones who can cope. Whatever life throws at them, they will always cope. On call twenty-four hours a day, seven days a week, whether their children are sick, their husbands are out of work or their parents are old and frail and need attending – they will cope . . . it can take enormous courage for women to admit that they cannot cope, that they may need help either from family and friends or the support systems . . . Frequently they will attempt to survive it alone, falling helplessly into a deeper and darker depression as they feel more and more trapped by the life they are leading. As their world closes in on them, their self-esteem evaporates into a haze of loneliness and desperation as they retreat further and further from those who could help them.' As the papers were quick to point out, she was 'speaking from the heart', as someone who had experienced some of this distress.

A woman's age

Depression can strike at any age as witnessed by the following accounts.

Coline, now aged eighteen, recalls that around the age of fourteen or fifteen she began to feel: 'Useless, physically unattractive. Some mornings I woke up and felt mentally like crap. I had to decide what to wear and I might change six times because I felt so bad about how I looked. I didn't like me and the easiest way to change that, I guess I thought then, was to change the way I looked.'

Sheila is twenty-four and, two years out of university, is working for a publishing company. 'In my last year at university, I split up from my boyfriend. It was a mutual decision but that didn't stop me being seriously depressed for several months afterwards. I couldn't stop crying or talking about it. Seeing couples really upset me. I had been very self-confident before but all that went, I felt I wasn't interesting, that I had nothing to say. And, of course, without a man, I no longer felt I was attractive.'

Need I add that both these young women are highly intelligent and very attractive. Yet both suffer from depression linked to low self-esteem and low self-confidence. Intelligence and good looks are no protection against depression.

At forty-five, Leslie was reasonably content. She had worked in marketing, quite successfully, for fifteen years; she owned her own house, had a good income and a nice boyfriend. But when she was made redundant and stayed unemployed for several months, everything changed. 'Though intellectually I knew that many people were being made redundant and that it often took six months to find another job, I felt completely worthless, inadequate, suicidal at times. It seemed my whole life was a failure. Not only could I not hold down a decent job but I'd never married, never had children. My boyfriend was OK, and supportive enough, but I wasn't madly in love, nor was he, so that seemed like another failure too.'

Jennifer was sixty when she discovered her husband had been having a long affair with another woman. He told her about it, said it was over, and assumed they could continue their lives as before. She was deeply upset, and felt she had lived a sham of a marriage. He refused to discuss the affair with her or, more importantly, explain why he had had an affair and what that might have said about their marriage. In her misery and constant turmoil, she began to doubt herself, her abilities, above all her sexuality and her attractiveness.

Why we get depressed

Often the obvious and immediate cause of depression is the loss of a significant relationship, or an important aspect of life such as work. Perhaps the 'hidden' depression is most likely to strike (and statistics in the 1995 report *Social Focus on Women* support this view)[5] when a woman is busy with home and work. She may feel overwhelmed by the workload or, rather, workloads and be acutely aware that she is losing herself, her very essence, in the process of looking after other people. In a recent novel by American writer Anne Tyler, *Ladder of Years*, the heroine Delia feels so overwhelmed by her family and so taken for granted that she just leaves and goes to another town where she starts another life. She feels justified in her actions when she reads the description her family has given the police: '. . . Mrs Grinstead stands

5′2″ or possibly 5′6″ and weighs either 90 or 110 pounds. Her eyes are blue or gray or perhaps green.'

There is conflicting research on whether single women are mentally (and physically) healthier than their married sisters. But I have interviewed plenty of single women who seem to have it all – almost – but are often depressed.

Twenty-four-year-old Gina has a busy social life and numerous admirers. She looks and dresses like a model. One morning, as yet another lover departs, she breaks down and cries uncontrollably. She doesn't want this sort of life. She expects something better; she is, after all, Daddy's girl, his little princess. But other men don't treat her that way. Most of the time, she is screaming inside. She'd give up a lot for security and peace of mind.

Jean is in her mid thirties, climbing the ladder of a large corporation. She chose to take part in a brief course on career development. At first, she was aggressive, deploring the fact the group were all women and protesting she couldn't do certain tasks. But by the mid afternoon of the first day, she had admitted how miserable she was, that she felt she was falling apart, that one day she might do something crazy in the supermarket and let herself down. She was living with a man who had left her for another woman on more than one occasion. He was rude and emotionally abusive to her. She was drinking heavily and this was taking its toll on her appearance. She complained of the anguish of trying to hold herself together. 'I feel I am wearing a mask and it will break up any day.'

There are also those of us who lead a double life, as men have always done. Some married women will have an affair because they just want a sexual adventure. But many will risk this because they are not happy or fulfilled enough in their relationship. They will often say the affair makes them feel 'real', that their lover is more affectionate, more caring, more celebrating of them, than their husband. It is certainly a less passive way of dealing with the depression of life, but usually an affair only exacerbates our pain and anger, and our underlying depression remains.

There are conditions such as anorexia, or other psycho-somatic illnesses, which are another way in which we can express our deep psychic distress. Eating disorders are particularly common among women and girls; children of only seven and eight have been found to suffer from anorexia. See Chapter 5 to explore this more fully.

What triggers depression

We often recognise that the apparent and immediate cause of our depression is loss – loss of a relationship, loss of work, loss of health through illness, loss through change. Major life events, even those which might seem ones to celebrate such as marriage, moving house, or a holiday, can cause their own emotional turmoil. Another cause is anticipated loss, the fear that your partner may leave you, the terrible insecurity of knowing you may be made redundant, or anxiety about money.

But any event, any loss, is almost always complicated by the context in which it happens. Depression is inevitable during and after marriage breakdown, for example, but how serious it is and how long it lasts (in whatever form, overt or hidden) will depend on many factors, including our financial and work status, support network of friends and family, physical health, and our earliest experiences of relationships. Everyone's self-esteem is knocked by a relationship not working, but it may be harder to recover if you have previously experienced similar events. For example, the divorce or death of parents can make the child in later life more at risk of a broken marriage, and more vulnerable to depression afterwards. Similarly, present day experiences will also resonate.

> When Anne was divorced, it did not help that through work, she found herself in a strange town. She had never been very gregarious, but here she was friendless. It underlined her feelings of loneliness, of failure, that she could never succeed in relationships.

Psychologist Dorothy Rowe wrote an article for the *Mail on Sunday* in which she explained that depression often arises from: '. . . a serious discrepancy between what we thought our life is [or should be?] and what it actually is.'[6] We 'fall apart' when we acknowledge that discrepancy, or because something in our lives makes us acknowledge it. Whether aged twenty-two or forty-two a heterosexual woman will feel she has 'failed as a real woman' if she is not in a permanent relationship with a man. This is what was, and is, expected of her. In the same way, a woman in her late thirties may feel she has not succeeded because she took time out from her career to look after a family, and is now finding it hard to return to the mainstream of work.

Sigmund Freud, the 'father' of psychoanalysis, stressed how vital love and work are to our wellbeing. But why do we so often have such high expectations of those areas of our lives that if we 'fail' or don't live up to those expectations, we feel so negative about ourselves? This is the million dollar question. Why do some people, especially women, suffer more depression because they feel failures at living? Why do some of us never fully recover our emotional wellbeing after a bereavement or divorce? Why are some of us apparently so frightened of life that we withdraw and constantly court depression? Why do some of us feel so discontented with ourselves that we try to starve ourselves to death through anorexia, whilst some of our fatter sisters are fairly happy and contented?

Nature or nurture?

There used to be two clearly distinct schools of thought about the causes of depression – the biological and the psychological. The strictly biological argument was that depression arises from a disturbance within the patient's nervous system. It is a physical disorder and can therefore be dealt with by physical treatments such as drugs or ECT electric shock treatment. In the biological or organic approach, particular emphasis is laid by psychiatrists on the role of physiological, genetic and biochemical factors.

The main psychological approach, originating from the seminal work of analysts Freud and Jung (see below), is that of psychoanalysis and psychotherapy. It recognises the lasting effect of early childhood experiences and conflicts, and the difficulties encountered during critical stages of development. Through psychotherapy, the person is enabled to make conscious, and to understand, unconscious emotions and conflicts, and thereby resolve them.

The other two psychological schools are those of behaviour therapy and cognitive therapy. Both are based on learning theory, with the view that we can unlearn 'bad' habits which cause symptoms such as depression or anxiety. Strict behaviourists would not take into account the effects of unconscious processes or past events. They argue that depression is caused by a lack of rewards, and linked to this, that we become depressed because we feel we have no control over our lives, that we are helpless.

Cognitive therapy, a more recent offshoot of behaviour therapy, has been shown to be quite successful in treating depression. It argues that we become depressed because of the way we view and think about the world. When depressed, we have negative thoughts and a pessimistic view of life. Cognitive therapists aim to remove depression by helping the person to change her attitudes and ways of thinking, by exchanging negative for positive thoughts.

Although drugs (that is, biological treatments) are still commonly used by doctors to treat depression, there is a greater acceptance by the medical establishment that psychological factors are involved. This is partly the influence of the holistic movement as well as that of psychotherapy, but also in large part because of the increasing awareness of the effect of psychological factors on physical illness, such as cancer, and an increased understanding of conditions such as anorexia which seem to be wholly psychosomatic.

The medical establishment is slowly beginning to recognise the link between body and mind. A joint statement from the Royal College of Psychiatrists and the Royal College of General Practitioners (for their Defeat Depression campaign) states that: '. . . depression has a range of causes including major stressful life events, bereavement, divorce or separation, loss of social support and close relationships, physical illnesses, genetic factors, biochemical changes in the brain.'

When someone becomes depressed, clearly there is a biochemical reaction in the brain, and this reaction can be changed by treatment to eliminate the depression. But what should come first? The new wonder drug Prozac works on the levels of a substance called serotonin in the brain. It is believed that low levels of serotonin cause depression. Put simply, Prozac and other SSRIs (selective serotonin re-uptake inhibitors) prevent the levels of serotonin falling. It certainly seems to be a very successful anti-depressant drug for many people. However, once you stop taking Prozac, the depression may return (perhaps months or years later)

because the underlying causes (which triggered the biochemical response) have not been dealt with. Interestingly,
some psychiatrists and psychotherapists are finding that they
can usefully combine psychotherapy with prescribing SSRI
drugs such as Prozac, because these drugs don't sedate
people or make them less responsive to therapy.

Hormones

Hormones obviously play their part in people's emotional
dramas, and especially in women's. We experience more
hormonal changes throughout life than men – puberty,
menstrual cycles, pregnancy, menopause. But it is the
old question of the chicken and the egg, or what comes
first? Women are not 'ruled' by their hormones as many
men, including doctors, have suggested. Whether or not a
woman finds her menopause difficult, for example, depends
on factors such as self-esteem, relationships, and the state of
her physical wellbeing. Changing levels of hormones such
as oestrogen do seem to have links with depression, but
there are also complicating social factors. Women at this
stage of life may feel less attractive, are afraid of ageing,
may be dealing with difficult teenagers and physically frail
parents. They are scared of a lonely old age. Women with a
history of depression are more likely to find the menopause
a difficult time emotionally.

At Turning Point's conference on Women and Mental
Health in June 1993, Dr Fiona Caldicott, a psychiatrist,
commented: 'There are several factors which are thought
to contribute to the excess of mental illnesses in women. It is
difficult to prove that biological and hormonal factors play a
part.' She believes that social factors are important, pointing
to the fact that women tend particularly to suffer from

depression between the ages of twenty-five and forty-five when most are having children: 'It is not helpful that young women are presented with a glamorised view of both marriage and motherhood in a society which probably contributes to deeper feelings of disappointment when the typical realities impinge.'

In commenting that depression is twice as common among women as among men, the Royal College of Psychiatrists and the Royal College of General Practitioners write: 'The reasons are complex and probably include both social stress factors (particularly the vulnerability of women with young children to additional stresses or difficulties) and hormonal factors.'

Can depression be healthy?

I believe that depression is often a normal, healthy reaction to something happening in our lives, mediated by earlier experiences and emotions. It becomes unhealthy when repeated, time and time again, as a pattern of reaction to problems and setbacks: when we don't listen to our depression to understand what it is telling us, for example when we stay in the wrong relationship or the wrong job. But when we do try to listen to the 'message', through self-exploration whether on our own or through professional help such as therapy and self-understanding, we can work towards change – healthy change.

Alice Miller, a psychoanalyst, puts it beautifully in *The Drama of Being a Child*[7]: 'Our true, repressed history is stored up in our body, which attempts to recount it and to be listened to, by way of symptoms. This is in fact for our own well-being, as denial is highly destructive to the adult. . . . As soon as the truth can be slowly explored, thanks to the conscious experience of once-repressed feelings, the language of symptoms becomes superfluous. They often simply disappear.'

In *The Road Less Travelled* Dr M. Scott Peck takes this insight further and explains that depression springs from an awareness, often unconscious, that change is necessary and that change entails giving up some of the 'old self'.[8] 'Since mentally healthy human beings must grow, and since giving up or loss of the old self is an integral part of the process of mental and spiritual growth, depression is a normal and basically healthy phenomenon.' But many of the patients he has treated do not understand what is happening to them, they just want to rid themselves of the terrible symptoms of depression: 'They do not know that things can no longer be "the way they used to be". But the unconscious knows. It is precisely because the unconscious in its wisdom knows that "the way things used to be" is no longer tenable or constructive that the process of growing and giving up is begun on an unconscious level and depression is experienced.'

But once this process of growing and giving up becomes a conscious one, we can become angry rather than depressed; active rather than passive; empowered, not powerless. We may value ourselves for the first time, and thus encourage others to value us. We won't always be happy but we will be mentally more healthy, more able to deal with life. In *A Dictionary of Mental Health* Richard B. Fisher makes the point that: 'Mental health probably entails a fair amount of unhappiness, a consequence of the perpetual need to solve life's problems.'[9]

Sigmund Freud said all he aimed to do through psycho-analysis was to turn neurotic misery into ordinary unhappi-ness. But Carl Jung, the Swiss psychiatrist who broke with

Freud to develop his own ideas on analysis, had a more spiritual approach to analysis, and saw its goal as making people whole. He believed that neurotic symptoms such as depression appear when we feel 'stuck', when life seems meaningless and empty. It may well be that our lives are unbalanced, with work given such a great priority that our personal lives are suffering, if not non-existent. It is once again about being true to ourselves, our very essence.

Jung saw depression, or other forms of psychic distress, as an opportunity for healing, for getting in touch with the real 'self'. This isn't as airy-fairy as it may sound. So many women (and not a few men) have always put partners and families first, and denied themselves – not treats, nothing so superficial, but perhaps denied using their intellect, furthering their education, their potential. Women are always adapting themselves to others, as homeopath Sohani Gonzalez explains: 'If not to partners, then to children or parents or colleagues at work.' Similarly, the classic career woman may have denied her nurturing side by putting all her energy into succeeding at work.

Filling the emptiness

Jung believed you could achieve 'breakthrough' by 'break-down'. Nicola Haskyns is a transpersonal psychotherapist, who works in a holistic way and very much agrees with Jung's philosphy: 'I and my colleagues believe that we should work with someone's crisis, that every crisis has a purpose. I think a part of you brings about the crisis in order to do something about it, or because being depressed does something for you. This means we have to work together with the depression, to accept it and move on from there.'

Whether or not a particular event such as divorce or

redundancy brings someone into therapy, Nicola Haskyns finds that everyone talks about a spiritual emptiness, a lack of connectedness to other parts of themselves (although they may not be so clear in the way they express it): 'They all talk about a hole, an empty feeling inside. As they talk, I realise everyone has their way of filling the emptiness, whether with alcohol, or relationships which don't work, or a career. We all get in such a panic about filling in time.' Psychodynamic psychotherapist Jill Curtis echoes this: 'I see so many women suppressing their emotions, their anger. They often smoke a lot, to fill the emptiness. I ask them, "What is going up in smoke? Why do you need a smokescreen round you?"'

> Maria is a teacher in her late forties. She has lived through years of a miserable marriage, a difficult divorce, being a single parent, coping on a very low income. She has been depressed many times, and has experienced some counselling and has done the strenuous work of self-analysis. 'Now I understand my depression. I don't exactly welcome it but I know it is telling me something is wrong in my life, but I don't want to change it. It is about coming to terms with the need to change. Now I'm more able to reflect, to ask Why? What must I do? Before I understood this, I was terrified when I became depressed. I thought I was going mad, that I would end up in a mental hospital. Now I recognise depression is part of a process.'

Maria's experience shows that depression can be positive and a way to effect lasting change, even though it may be extremely painful when we are living through it. As therapist Jill Curtis says: 'It can be appropriate to be depressed.'

Living in the present

Western society places a constant stress on the future. We are plagued by anxieties and fears about what is to come.

Jung wrote: 'People in the modern world are always living so that something better is to happen tomorrow, always in the future, so they don't begin to live their lives. They are up in the head. When a man (*sic*) begins to know himself, to discover the roots of his past in himself, it is a new way of life.'

There is an old Sanskrit saying which perfectly illustrates the importance of living in the present:

Look to this day
For it is Life
The very Life of Life
In its brief course lie all
The realities and truths of existence
The joy of growth
The splendour of action
The glory of power.
For yesterday is but a memory
And tomorrow is only a vision
But today well lived
Makes every yesterday a memory of happiness
And every tomorrow a vision of hope
Look well therefore to this day.

Kalidasa

This isn't entirely true, but if we spend too much time worrying about the future – or the past – we are not living today to the full.

Breaking through the stereotypes

Women today are still brought up to fit into traditional female roles (see Chapter 2). We are encouraged to be sweet and 'fluffy', as one young woman commented, and to be passive, nurturing, unadventurous. Research has shown that a high degree of sex-stereotyped behaviour in women correlated with high levels of anxiety, low self-esteem and generally poor emotional adjustment: 'In contrast, women with an androgynous identity (i.e. both "masculine" and "feminine" characteristics) were found to be more outgoing, creative and successful professionally.'[10]

Psychodynamic psychotherapist Jill Curtis agrees: 'I see so many women, and some men too, who have lost the sense of "who am I?"' She believes that depression is an expression of disease. It is telling us that we are not being true to ourselves, to the whole of ourselves. We are particularly prone to suffer from this as women, trying to fit ourselves into the model expected of us from an early age.

> Louise had always been a great day-dreamer, like so many women. She thought of the wonderful man she would marry, the children she would have, the amazing career. A reasonable career did materialise but by the age of forty-two, despite several offers of marriage, she hadn't found her Prince Charming and she was still childless. She had also regularly suffered from depression because she felt she had failed to achieve the 'right' things in life. She began to have psychotherapy and gradually she realised how much time and energy she had wasted in dreaming about the future, not appreciating what she had, being depressed. It was part of her running away from her perfectly acceptable, untraumatic and deeply bourgeois upbringing (she'd never been abused as a child, just bored).

Despite being a talented and resourceful person, Louise felt a failure because she had not achieved the 'normal' goals – marriage and children. In therapy, she learned that this was partly because she hadn't wanted to: she was, perhaps unconsciously, rebelling against the stereotyping. Conflict was therefore inevitable between her rebellious side and her conventional side. Once she confronted this, she was able to understand the conflict and work towards resolving it.

The power of dreams

Dreams can be an important aspect of self-exploration, of contacting the real self. Therapists frequently work with dreams.

> Joanna had come through a period of great turmoil, a powerful relationship which had ended disastrously and a period of unemployment. She had become seriously depressed, and a mix of therapy and anti-depressants had eventually helped her through it. One night she had a dream which helped her to feel whole again, that she could put the past behind her and concentrate on living. She dreamt that she was in an operating theatre. She was terrified because 'they' were going to give her a new face. She was terrified of the pain but even more so because she knew she would never feel comfortable with the new face, however beautiful it made her. 'I knew in the dream that I couldn't live with the new me, the new persona. I would always know what lay underneath.'

Joanna realised that the dream was telling her to be true to herself, to stop pretending in order to atract someone or find work. The relief of understanding this was enormous. She felt stronger, clearer about her strengths *and* her weaknesses, and about what she hoped for from life and herself.

You can only be true to yourself if you learn to value yourself, to accept and be realistic about your strengths and your weaknesses. You also have to understand that when someone criticises or compliments you, they may have their own reasons for this. They may be trying to undermine you, for example. Women seem to find this particularly difficult.

They depend on other people for approbation. They see themselves reflected in the emotions and behaviour of others. They do not always see themselves clearly; there may be years, even decades, of other people's views and comments obscuring the true picture.

Defining self-esteem

Research confirms that women in every age group have appallingly low levels of self-esteem. Low self-esteem is a major cause of depression. As Dr Caldicott said at the Turning Point conference: 'We know that feelings of self-esteem are crucial to good psychological functioning . . .'

It is vital, and healthy, to realise that there are many aspects of women's lives which can, and often do, undermine self-esteem and therefore create depression – feelings of powerlessness; loss of control; physical, emotional and sexual abuse. Not that such experiences don't depress men, just that many will not experience them at all, or rarely. It is not insignificant that there is serious depression, and suicide, among unemployed men, underlining the fact that employment gives you status and the respect of others, as well as self-respect. Psychologist Bernice Andrews, who has done a great deal of research into depression among women, pointed to the parallel between depressed women and unemployed men. In this situation men experience very similar feelings of low self-esteem to women.

I am sure it is not insignificant that the words or phrases women use to describe their depressed state so often reveal feelings of powerlessness, imprisonment, lack of energy. They talk about feeling immobilised, disabled, and unable to function.

'I feel trapped.'

'I feel a great weight, pressure, bearing down on me, it's almost physically painful, but I can't run away from it because it is part of me.'

'I feel I've lost my way.'

'Everything in me slows down, I'm sluggish mentally, physically, emotionally.'

American author and psychotherapist Dr Nathaniel Branden, a leading expert on self-esteem, writes: 'I cannot think of a single psychological problem – from anxiety and depression, to underachievement at school or at work, to fear of intimacy, happiness or success, to alcohol or drug abuse, to spouse battering or child molestation, to co-dependency and sexual disorders, to passivity and chronic aimlessness, to suicide and crimes of violence – that is not traceable, at least in part, to the problem of deficient self-esteem.'[11]

So what exactly is self-esteem? Why is it so important to our mental health and wellbeing? Dr Branden explains that self-esteem is: '. . . a profound and powerful human need, essential to healthy adaptiveness, that is, to optimal functioning and self-fulfilment.' He defines self-esteem as: '. . . the experience that we are appropriate to life and to the requirements of life . . . It is confidence in our ability to think, confidence in our ability to cope with the basic challenges of life, and confidence in our right to be successful and happy, the feeling of being worthy, deserving, entitled to assert our needs and wants, achieve our values, and enjoy the fruits of our efforts.'

Put simply, self-esteem is valuing ourselves and having confidence in our abilities, reactions, emotions. If we respect ourselves, others are more likely to show us respect. As a male friend said to me once, commenting on a woman who was constantly complaining about her weight and her body shape, 'Why should I find her attractive if she doesn't like herself?'

Dr Branden calls self-esteem 'the immune system of consciousness'. Just as our physical health depends on our immune system, the body's natural defences, to fight off infection, so our mental health depends on our self-esteem to protect us against 'neuroses' such as depression or anxiety. Lack of, or low, self-esteem affects our mental and emotional functioning. This in due course may lead to depression, which can also affect our immune system and make us physically ill. The links between mind and body are strong, giving rise to psychosomatic illnesses such as eating disorders or stress-related conditions.

A seminal work on women and depression is *Social Origins of Depression* by George Brown and Tirril Harris. They studied a group of women in Camberwell, South London, investigating the reasons for their depression. They concluded that low self-esteem was an important factor in causing depression among these women. They wrote: '. . . a person's ongoing self-esteem is crucial in determining whether generalised hopelessness develops – that is, response to loss and disappointment is mediated by a sense of one's own ability to control the world and thus to repair damage . . . if self-esteem and feelings of mastery are low *before* a major loss or disappointment, a woman is less likely to be able to imagine herself emerging from her privation.'[12]

The roots of self-esteem

Obviously a number of factors contribute to our image of ourselves, our self-esteem, our sense of worth. It is as if, from the moment of conception, our psyche is like a piece of stone, being sculpted by more than one artist. On my notice-board, I have a photograph I took of a Rodin sculpture showing a naked woman half emerging from a piece of barely chiselled stone. That is how I see the emerging self, continually being shaped throughout life.

Our genetic inheritance is an important factor in determining our personality. Studies of identical twins separated at birth have shown striking similarities in their distinctive characters as adults. In one study which began in Minnesota in 1979, two men adopted by different families at birth were reunited some thirty-nine years later. They both bit their nails and suffered migraine headaches. Both smoked the same brand of cigarettes, drove the same kind of car, did the same sort of work, and both had woodworking as a hobby. Some of these researchers into genetic inheritance argue that as much as fifty per cent of our personality can be inherited.[13]

The other most significant shaper of our souls is our relationship with our parents, or parent figures, from day one of our lives, and some psychologists would argue from day one in the womb. There has been much controversial work on whether people remember hearing or feeling things when they were in their mother's womb. This is a fascinating idea and not one to be dismissed lightly, but I won't dwell on it here.

Early relationships

Every therapist I have spoken to stresses the fact that we can never underestimate the importance of our earliest relationships, and of early social conditioning. This belief is grounded in the work therapists have done with many distressed clients, and from their training in various theoretical schools. Sigmund Freud was the founder of psychoanalysis, the first 'talking treatment'. He discovered that through analysis, one can reveal unconscious conflicts and emotions which are causing various symptoms, whether physical or mainly psychological. These unconscious processes have, Freud argues, been suppressed since early childhood; our early impressions and experiences are retained throughout life, though often in the unconscious. Traumatic events or a loss, for example, divorce or bereavement, in adulthood may trigger off painful memories or suppressed desires from childhood.

Freud also believed that in our adult life we might repeat our infantile attachments and conflicts. He saw the past as inescapable, controlling us like a puppet master. In *Five Lectures* he wrote: 'You can regard psychoanalytic treatment as no more than a prolongation of education for the purpose of overcoming the residues of childhood.'

Following Freud, other analysts such as Melanie Klein, D. W. Winnicott and John Bowlby recognised the power of the past and of unconscious conflicts. But they put far more emphasis than Freud did on our early *relationships* with other people, especially parents or parent figures. For example, one of the most crucial stages for a child, argues Melanie Klein, is when she begins to recognise that she is 'separate' from her mother. She is both frightened and excited by this knowledge, as well as by realising that she can love and hate her mother. Klein explains that for most people these powerful childhood emotions are resolved. But if a parent goes into hospital, or dies, or leaves for no apparent reason, or is destructive either emotionally or physically to the child, she may believe that this is all her fault, that she has 'destroyed' her parent. This belief will be unconscious but the unconscious is powerful and those emotions may be triggered off years later, perhaps by losing someone close through death or divorce.

Uncovering our true selves

The group of analysts known as objects-relations theorists, including D.W. Winnicott and John Bowlby, argue that the main motivational drive in humans is to make relationships with other human beings. Only by developing healthy relationships, beginning with our parents, can we become mentally healthy. Within the safe and nurturing environment of such relationships we can develop our true 'self'. If such an environment is not provided in childhood, we will develop a false 'self' to protect ourselves against the feelings and fears of insecurity.

More recently, Alice Miller has written powerfully in *The Drama of Being a Child* about the effects on children of early experiences of neglect and abuse, whether emotional, sexual or physical: 'We are all prisoners of our childhood, whether we know it, suspect it, deny it, or have never even heard about the possibility.' She argues that: 'As children, we strive, above all else, to accommodate our parents' demands – spoken and unspoken; reasonable and unreasonable. In the process, we blind ourselves to our true needs and feelings. In our adult lives, this is like trying to sail a ship without a compass. Not knowing who we are, what we feel and what we need, even as grown-ups we remain subject to the expectations placed upon us from the very beginning of our lives, expectations we fulfilled not for love but for the illusion of love. Without that illusion, we could not have survived childhood.'[14]

Miller believes that these actions, this denying of one's true self, leaves a great emptiness. The 'person' who has accommodated himself or herself to parental needs cannot develop a true self: '. . . because he is unable to live it. Understandably, this person will complain of a sense of emptiness, futility, or homelessness, for the emptiness is real. A process of emptying, impoverishment, and crippling of his potential actually took place. The integrity of the child was injured when all that was alive and spontaneous in him was cut off.'

That crippled child will 'wear' a mask – the false self – in order to cope with other people's needs and demands. Some will never remove the mask, others will only in private or with people who make them feel secure. For some, the strain of being the false self becomes too great; some will become depressed, others know they need help but they are not sure why. For example, a therapist told me of one of her patients, a lively woman in her thirties, an artist, who came into therapy because she felt 'stuck'. As a child, her parents had divorced and she had put huge amounts of energy into 'oiling the wheels' of the family, before and after the divorce. She eventually realised through her therapy that most of her energy went into 'oiling the wheels' in all her relationships – with family, friends, lover – and she didn't have much left for herself.

Joan was also in her thirties when she realised therapy was a 'last resort' for her. For several years, her skin had been constantly peeling off, but none of the medical treatments she tried were successful. It was, explained her therapist, as if 'she couldn't stay in her own skin.' The reason why was tragic, and not uncommon. From an early age, Joan had been sexually abused by her father and she felt her life had been completely ruined. Her mother had remained distant, choosing not to 'see' what was happening between her husband and daughter. When Joan, as an adult, confronted her with the abuse, her mother admitted that she too had been abused in the same way by *her* father.

Before therapy, Joan had for the first time been in a relationship for several months and she felt confident enough to tell the man about the abuse. He left, thus reinforcing her feeling that she couldn't trust any man, and that she was completely worthless. She retreated from life; if she had to go out and walk down the street, she believed everyone was looking at her because they knew of her childhood secrets.

Terrible experiences in childhood, such as sexual or physical abuse, make women extremely vulnerable to depression. Psychologist Bernice Andrews explains: 'Depression will be chronic and recurrent. These women tend to blame themselves for what happened to them, and have very low self-esteem.' Joan's case is a tragic example of behaviour patterns being learned and repeated across two generations of the same family. As the poet Philip Larkin wrote in *This Be The Verse*: 'Man hands on misery to man.'

Learning Points

✔ Depression is often a healthy reaction to an event or experience in your life.

✔ Depression is telling you something is wrong, that you have become 'stuck'.

✔ Depression becomes unhealthy if you don't attend to the 'message' and try to work out what is wrong, and how you must deal with that.

✔ It is healthy to make changes, and depression is often linked to the need to change.

✔ Depression can give you the opportunity to make healthy changes, to get in touch with your real self, long obscured by your various roles as wife, mother, child and others.

✔ Your dreams can help you tune into what is causing your depression and help you understand which aspects of your life need changing.

✔ Low self-esteem often leads to depression.

✔ Many aspects of life can undermine your self-esteem – early conditioning, poor relationships with your parents, trauma or abuse in childhood.

2 Why Can't a Woman Be More Like a Man?

Why are women more prone to low self-esteem and therefore more depression? Almost every woman I know, however bright and attractive, admits to suffering from low self-esteem and a consequent lack of self-confidence quite regularly. Of course men suffer too, but they are far less likely to reveal it to other people, and possibly not even to themselves. And they have other ways of operating, as I'll discuss later, of setting aside psychological distress and getting on with their lives.

From early on, girls learn they are different from boys and, in some ways, inferior. However hard parents try to avoid discrimination and inequality between boys and girls, they cannot protect them from society's views. Inequality is still bred in the bones.

> What are little girls made of, made of?
> What are little girls made of?
> Sugar and spice
> And all things nice,
> That's what little girls are made of.
>
> What are little boys made of, made of?
> What are little boys made of?
> Frogs and snails
> And puppy-dog tails,
> That's what little boys are made of.

Research shows that parents, especially fathers, play differently with boys and girls, from the time they are small babies. Judy Mann, an American journalist, has written an interesting book on gender differences, *The Difference*, spurred on by watching her daughter deal with adolescence. She explains that numerous researchers have found that even in these apparently post-feminist times, parents are likely to encourage their daughters to play with dolls, and discourage their sons from doing so.[1]

Another study observed that boys received more positive responses than girls for playing with building blocks, and girls got more negative responses than boys for manipulating objects. Fathers tend to play much more roughly with their sons, tossing them in the air, encouraging adventure and derring-do. Baby girls are hugged, protected by their fathers.

It is more important for little girls to be clean, to have dry pants, to smell sweet. Girls are praised for being nice, neat, tidy. Boys are encouraged to play rough and tumble. Parents laugh indulgently when boys cover themselves with mud (and just watch the detergent ads to see who washes the filthy clothes afterwards). They like to see their daughters sitting quietly in a corner reading (which, ironically, is one reason girls often do better at reading and writing in school).

Even when parents try their hardest not to discriminate, giving girls lorries and boys dolls, for example, most girls still absorb, through some form of osmosis, society's views of the ideal image of femininity. Schoolteachers have different expectations of boys and girls; girls are given Barbie dolls and pretty clothes by aunts and grannies, even if not by their parents. If they don't conform, they may feel odd, different. And in children's eyes, and perhaps especially girls', that is a huge sin.

We can all remember an occasion when we have been

made to feel the outsider in the playground, when friends have gone off without us. It is a powerful emotion.

> Sylvia, now aged twenty-four, still remembers how, as a nine-year-old, she wore clothes from Oxfam shops and markets. This was typically the trendy thing to do for her well-educated, middle class parents' generation. But she mixed with many working-class girls at school who wore very expensive clothes: 'They called me a gypsy. I didn't like feeling so different.'

Social conditioning

Bernice Andrews is a psychologist who has done some major research studies into women and depression, and women with low self-esteem. She explains that from an early age women are socialised to be nurturers, always looking after other people. But we are also conditioned, by society if not by our families, to be passive: 'Women are rendered more helpless and subordinate than men during their lives.'

But surely, we might argue, it is different for young women growing up in the 1990s? Well, certainly there are far more attempts by parents and teachers to abandon the old stereotypes when bringing up girls and boys, but the media still gives out mixed messages. Models look increasingly anorexic, especially the young ones, while there are also women, often singers, who are loud and gutsy and outrageous – a mix of vamp and tomboy. Magazines for teenagers and young women print endless, and quite outspoken, articles on relationships and sex. But this can make the reader feel inadequate about her own experiences and feelings.

Body image

A 1995 report by the Health Education Authority revealed
that thirteen and fourteen-year-old girls suffered lower self-
esteem than their male counterparts.[2] This investigation was
carried out because, as the Foreword explains: 'Self esteem
is fundamental to young people's mental and emotional well
being and to their ability to realise their true potential.' The
researchers found that eighty-five per cent of boys described
themselves as confident compared with seventy-seven per
cent of girls. 'Boys . . . hold a markedly more positive self
image than girls do.' Girls, on the whole, worry more than
boys. 'Girls' most important aim is to be liked (71 per
cent compared to 47 per cent of boys) and admired, to be
acceptable, and popular with their peers. To achieve this,
how they look is felt to be of utmost importance.' Girls
admitted they were very sensitive about their appearance.
One girl (her background classified as AB) commented:
'I'm conscious about myself constantly – the way I look.
If I get spots I don't want to go out . . . and my weight, I'm
conscious of that all the time.'

The report stresses there are no significant regional or
social class variations in these views. Another girl (described
as C1C2) said: 'I had my hair cut and all I wanted was
for someone to say it looked nice, but when I asked
Adam, he said, "Actually it makes you look really old,
about forty-five". That really upset me and I went home
and cried.'

Apparently the boys were only too aware of how obsessed
girls are with their appearance: 'They perceive this as being
part of the girls' efforts to gain their approval, to "get a man"
. . .' We are talking about thirteen and fourteen-year-olds,
for goodness' sake, in the mid 1990s. These girls seem even
more anxious about their appearance than I and my friends
were thirty years ago.

It is not surprising that eating disorders such as anorexia seem to be reaching epidemic proportions. For not dissimilar reasons, smoking is on the increase among girls as young as nine. Commenting in July 1995 on a Government progress report on Health of the Nation targets, Gordon McVie, Scientific Director of the Cancer Research Campaign, said: 'We know that their [i.e. girls'] two main motivations are that cigarettes increase their self-esteem, and that they are used as a slimming device.'[3] Another health official quoted in the report (but unnamed) commented on the very negative images projected by the fashion industry: 'The vast majority of women are never going to be perfect in the fashion sense of the word. We must encourage everyone . . . to be more self-confident so that they do not make disastrous attempts to make themselves something they are not.'

I interviewed several teenage girls, and all spoke of their concerns about weight and looks, and how much less confident they felt if they didn't have a boyfriend. Unfortunately these feelings of low self-confidence and lack of self-esteem do not disappear as we grow older.

Sheila is seventeen: 'I don't feel normal if I'm not going out with someone. Having a boyfriend tells the world I'm OK.'

Miriam is sixteen years old: 'However well I'm doing at school, I cannot deal with emotional rejection. That knocks all my confidence and I become really depressed.'

At forty-nine, Janet is old enough to be the mother of these girls, but her feelings about relationships are very similar. She is a civil servant, a clever, pretty, gay woman. Several months ago, her twelve-year-old live-in relationship ended and she has felt fairly desperate since then: 'All I want is to be in a relationship. I have this great need to be the most important person to someone, especially as both my parents are dead and

I have no children. I have so little confidence if I'm not in a meaningful relationship.'

The double standard

When researching this book, almost every woman I spoke to, in all age groups, admitted they feel less valued, less confident, when they aren't involved in an emotional relationship. They all want 'someone special to me'.

Young women also have the double standard to confront, however sexually liberated they may feel. There is still a view, especially during the teenage years, that girls who are sexually active are 'sluts' and 'slags', while boys are 'studs'.

Similarly, despite the clarion calls from *Cosmopolitan* and other women's magazines, women are not expected to pursue men. A woman manager in her thirties, superconfident about work, will hesitate to call the man she rather fancied at the party last night. She explains: 'I'm supposed to wait until, or if, he calls. If a woman does the pursuing, it is assumed she is only after sex, not a relationship.'

Of course, it is not uncommon for women, from their teenage years onwards, to have many sexual relationships, which are often brief and unloving, because they do not value themselves. They are desperately searching for love, for identity. They may have been abused as children, or they may not have been brought up to think well of themselves. Psychotherapist Toni White speaks of the many women she sees with depression, always rooted in early pain: 'Unfortunately, women are brought up to be nice to other people, but not necessarily to themselves.'

A research study carried out by H.A. Moss and published in 1974 found that even at the tender age of seven weeks, girl babies were encouraged by their parents to smile and vocalise more than the boys. This suggests (rightly, I believe): '. . . the tendency of adult women to smile more than men – to be pleasant, to make the atmosphere around them pleasing – is one of the earliest lessons little girls are taught.'[4]

Fear of rejection

Women are reared to nurture and yet also to depend on others, supposedly a man. It is a curious message, especially when we consider that neither role, whether nurturing or being dependent, is much valued in today's society. In addition, we have all been conditioned to care about what other people may think about us.

The Health Education Authority study of self-esteem among thirteen- and fourteen-year-olds found that the biggest fear of all for girls is of rejection, of being disliked: 'They worry about standing out from the crowd, and conversely, gain confidence from being part of a peer group. Their fear of being conspicuous is reduced by attachment to a group, and many will go to great lengths to appear acceptable and avoid creating waves.' This fear of rejection is experienced by women of all ages, as the following examples illustrate.

Jan is forty-five, working in personnel: 'I'm far too dependent on other people's opinions of me. I can feel very low if I'm rejected – or perceive myself to have been rejected. And I always assume it's because of something *I've* done.'

Kate is forty-nine, a teacher who was married, mostly unhappily, for thirteen years. She has been single for seven: 'It has taken me almost all this time to realise *I* mattered too, that I had some rights in the marriage. But I was brought up in a way that didn't encourage that. When I was small, I was my father's pretty little fairy. He went to Paris and brought me back lovely dresses. He liked showing me off, but I was definitely to be seen and not heard. As I became older, he found me difficult because I would speak my mind. He hated that. And even though he didn't like my husband, who had affairs, he blamed the break-up of the marriage on me.'

The more I researched this book, the angrier I have become about the way we have been conditioned as women. It is great to have more opportunities at work, to be liberated in many ways. But the confidence to use those opportunities, to fulfil our potential as women, is too often lacking because of early experiences. We need stronger foundations if we are to develop a strong sense of our own self-worth.

Cultural cripplers

Dr Nathaniel Branden writes in *'The Six Pillars of Self-Esteem'* that: '. . . many an adult in psychotherapy complains of still hearing the internalised voices of Mother or Father telling them they are "bad", "rotten", "stupid", "worthless".'[5] It's certainly the case that some women do struggle against such memories coldly inscribed on their psyches, but many have had perfectly reasonable relationships with their parents. The early knocks to our self-esteem are often less specific, more subversively received from many areas of society.

'There are many cultural cripplers of girls and enablers of boys,' writes Judy Mann in *The Difference*. 'There is much that remains to be done before women and girls can feel safe in our culture, before they can feel they are as valued and valuable to society as men are. The undermining of girls and the false empowering of boys at the expense of girls begins at a much earlier age than previously thought . . . For girls much of their early adult life [and I would add, for some much longer] is one of recovery, of getting back on their feet, of trying to become whole again . . . What would happen to girls if they were not robbed of their "selves"? If they were raised to be independent, self sufficient women? What would happen if boys were raised to respect girls as equals, to listen to their voices, and to value them as friends?'[6]

I'll hazard a guess – or, rather, lay a large bet: we wouldn't suffer so much depression, we would be angrier about our lives and the injustices we have to suffer, because we would value ourselves more. For, as Dr Branden writes: 'Of all the judgements we pass in life, none is as important as the one we pass on ourselves.'[7]

Having high self-esteem does not equal selfishness, nor does it mean having an unbearably high opinion of ourselves. Part of valuing ourselves and our abilities is respecting other people and their needs and abilities.

Women can be the harshest judges of themselves. Many of us have several 'degrees' in self criticism and guilt. I heard many comments like these during the course of my research:

'It doesn't take much to make me feel worthless, and guilt always does it.'

'I don't like myself. Why should anyone else?'

'When I feel guilty, which is regularly, then I feel depressed and powerless, blaming myself for everything.'

Psychologist Bernice Andrews has for many years studied the factors which make women more vulnerable to depression: 'My hypothesis is, that when bad things happen, men blame women and women blame themselves.'

A young woman I spoke to who worked, whilst a student,

as a volunteer in a Rape Crisis Centre deplored the fact that almost every woman who has been raped blames herself. And of course, this self-blaming by rape victims is reinforced by our legal system and the often unfortuante comments made by judges.

Mothers and daughters

Dr Branden writes that: 'The proper aim of parental nurturing is to prepare a child for independent survival as an adult. An infant begins in a condition of total dependency. If his or her (*sic*) upbringing is successful, the young man or woman will have evolved out of that dependency into a self-respecting and self-responsible human being who is able to respond to the challenges of life competently and enthusiastically.'[8]

This is the counsel of perfection but, in truth, most parents are less clear-cut, more muddled, in the upbringing of their children. They themselves may not have experienced good parenting and so find it difficult not to repeat old patterns. Philip Larkin's bitter poem *This Be The Verse* is painfully nearer the truth for many people:

> They fuck you up, your mum and dad.
> They may not mean to, but they do.
> They fill you with the faults they had
> And add some extra, just for you.
>
> But they were fucked up in their turn
> By fools in old-style hats and coats,
> Who half the time were soppy-stern
> And half at one another's throats . . .

A child's early relationship with her mother is critical to her later development of identity and self-esteem. Psychiatrists

Pamela Ashurst and Zaida Hall explain in *Understanding Women in Distress* that before a child is aware of her gender, she must form her 'basic primary identity', her 'true self', which enables the child to experience herself 'as an effective, emotional and interpersonal agent'.[9] Early on, we learn trust and security from our mothers; we feel accepted and loved. If a child doesn't feel this 'unconditional' love from her mother, then she will feel she is not good enough, not, as the case may be, that the mother is not a good enough mother.

Volumes have been written on the mother/child relationship. This is obviously because in most societies, mothers are the dominant nurturer and protector of the baby, though experts such as John Bowlby have argued that a man has the capacity to be as effective a mother figure as a woman.

The Health Education Authority study of young teenagers found that parents are an important source of self-esteem for both sexes: '. . . with mothers and female relatives being rather more important than fathers and male relatives.' Boys said they received more positive reinforcement from their fathers than girls reported. In fact, one in ten girls said their fathers did not make them feel good about themselves.

Theories abound about the importance of the relationship between mother and daughter (see the Book List at the back of this book). It has been suggested by American writer Nancy Chodorow that mothers find it difficult to separate themselves from their daughters, because they are the same gender. Daughters find this closeness threatening – the way their mothers seem to know them 'too well', for example – and this often results in the alternating closeness and hostility between the two, especially during adolescence. Our mothers can seem too close, too all-knowing.

We gain our sense of identity and self-worth from both parents but it does seem that the relationship with the mother is more crucial, or certainly in a society where inequality

between the sexes remains. It is hard for mothers: they want
to protect and nurture their daughters; they want them to
fulfil their potential, and to have a rich, enjoyable life;
they will worry about the dangers, the sexual risks, and
the risks of exploitation. Mothers' concerns for their sons
will tend to be different; boys can be allowed to be more
adventurous.

The search for approval

Feminist therapists Louise Eichenbaum and Susie Orbach
have written that: 'women are not to be the main actors
in their lives. That is, they are not brought up to be
autonomous, but instead are always deferring to others.'
Mothers recognise this and, whilst they want to cherish
their daughters, they also feel they cannot completely do so
because their daughters too will eventually have to put their
own needs second. So Eichenbaum and Orbach argue that
inside every woman is a little girl whose need for nurturing
was never wholly met. This inevitably leads to a lack of
self-esteem.[10]

These feelings are passed on from generation to generation, especially by mothers who have very low self-esteem.
These women will have to be especially strong and brave to
prevent themselves undermining their daughters' self-worth.
Women compete with their daughters for the attention of
their husbands, particularly when the marriage is not a good
one, and/or when their own sense of identity and sexuality
are not sound. It is hard for them not to pass on their own
insecurities.

> Gillian is seventeen, a young woman who, despite good academic
> results, is mainly concerned about finding a boyfriend: 'That is
> what gives me confidence in myself, and I know I've got it from
> my mother. She is always looking to a man to provide her with
> security.'

Even when women recall their father's affection and unconditional approval, they will say it was not enough to counter the disapproval they felt from their mother.

> Sarah is forty-five: 'My father adored me, and has made me feel strong and beautiful. But despite that, I can often feel depressed and powerless. I feel as if I spent a lot of my childhood trying to please my mother, and so sometimes I feel as if I have no sense of myself as an independent person. She wasn't very pleased with me. I'm not imagining this, my sister agrees and says her relationship with our mother was fine and straightforward.'
>
> Sarah was the clever child and she believes her mother was in competition with her all the time, and so was always criticising her: 'My grandfather, that is, my father's father, thought I was wonderful and my mother resented this because she had not had a father since a young age. She somehow felt I was taking her place. No-one ever said she was clever, though she was. I felt she unequivocally loved my sister but it was much more complicated for me. She said I showed off a lot, and would make that awful comment, which her mother had made to her, 'Who do you think is going to look at you then?' I have always cried a lot and this exasperated my mother. I felt she observed me, rarely consoled me. My husband does the same. I married my mother.'

Not surprisingly, there are some problems with the marriage. Sarah has experienced bouts of depression, especially over relationships with men. But she has spent useful time, including some counselling, analysing the reasons. Thus she can look back to her childhood and comment on her difficult relationship with her mother.

> 'We are on the whole a very different generation because we do look at ourselves, our feelings. My mother did not reflect much. She was very much of the generation that "got on and did".'

Setting examples

Consciously or unconsciously, our mothers furnish us with

a role model in our relationships, especially in marriage. Obviously there are generational differences; women aged forty plus, especially those who are middle-class, have usually experienced a fairly traditional family life, with a non-working mother (or certainly while the children were small) and a father who did little in the house. Of course, every family has its unique differences – the father who loved cooking, the mother who did all the decorating – but, to quote Tolstoy in Anna Karenina: 'All happy families resemble one another, but each unhappy family is unhappy in its own way.'

> Kate is a forty-nine-year-old teacher who was seriously depressed for most of her twelve-year marriage, and for several years afterwards. I wondered why she hadn't sought help – counselling or therapy, for example. She explained: 'I thought I should be able to sort things out for myself. I couldn't tell my family because we never talked about that sort of thing. We were brought up to soldier on, whatever was happening to us. My mother was an absolute martyr. She told me more than once that she never said a bad word about her kids to her friends. So she had to bottle everything up. In the same way, she hated raised voices, arguments, expressions of powerful emotions ... I think I and my brothers have all been fairly dysfunctional. We weren't encouraged to look at ourselves. I wasn't meant to promote myself, to have ideas, especially above my station. 'When I went to marriage guidance counselling, the counsellor asked me, "What do you want?" To think what *I* might want seemed like a sin. It's a wonderful freedom now to realise I can ask that, even though I may not always get what I want.'

Daughters appear to feel more guilt about their mothers than sons do, probably because they identify more with them, as Janet's story illustrates.

> Janet's mother died only a few months after Janet finally accepted that she was gay, and moved in with another woman: 'I could never have told my mother I was gay, she would have been

very upset. I remember that in my late teens, I had a very intense, though non-sexual, relationship with another woman. My mother then got very angry. I had a very close, emotional relationship with my mother, classic love/hate. I felt guilty about this, and yet resentful too. From an early age, I had to do more in the house than my two brothers. I always knew she would have been quite happy if she had had a third boy instead of me. She once told me, in a rather matter-of-fact way, that it was easier emotionally to have boys. I still think it is better to produce a boy.'

But it was Janet who regularly visited her mother after her father's death: 'I used to get very depressed on these visits, we'd cry a lot together. I felt sorry for my mother because she was so miserable, so lonely, she had no job to provide some structure to her life, no energy. I suppose I felt guilty too. But I was also lonely, living on my own without a decent relationship. At that time I didn't realise I was gay. I suppose I needed her. I forget how awful things were, how desperate.'

Having your own child

Women's feelings about their mothers are often heightened when they themselves become mothers. In the mid 1990s, it is especially hard because, as psychiatrists Ashurst and Hall explain '. . . motherhood has become a lonely condition, when responsibility for the sole care of another human being, the baby, may be experienced as overwhelming and burdensome in its isolation. If her own experience of being mothered has been inadequate to prepare her for the task of mothering her own child, if her life experiences have been such that her sense of self has been battered and her self-esteem lowered, and if her partner is unwilling to give the support she needs . . . a woman is most likely to become depressed.'[11] Having a child inevitably changes, if not threatens, our sense of self, as Maria's experience demonstrates.

Maria, a lively woman who practises complementary massage,

gave birth to her much wanted son at the age of thirty-seven. Her partner had not been keen to have a child but had finally come to terms with the idea. After a good pregnancy, Maria experienced a very painful and difficult labour: 'Physically I felt as if I'd been hit by a bus. I had a terrible sense of panic, realising I couldn't run away from the baby. I was responsible for him. As a child, I had been claustrophobic at school and frequently truanted.

'It was the first time in my life I couldn't run away from a difficult situation. I felt very vulnerable inside, I wanted mothering myself. I was supposed to be in bliss and joy, but deep down I was panicky and miserable. I knew I shouldn't feel like this. My partner couldn't cope and retreated into himself and his work.

'I found it very difficult to ask for help, I suppose that's very female, isn't it? I also found, and still do find, looking back at my own childhood very painful. I was born several years after my siblings. My mother and I were sort of a separate package. She was very needy of me, we had a very intense relationship. Yet when my son was born, I didn't feel responsible enough to look after him. I wanted to be looked after, I felt only about four myself.

'Sometimes my relationship with my mother was quite claustrophobic. It's scary to look at what there is of her inside me, to remember the way she brought me up. She's a great worrier and she passed on a lot of that to me. I feel very vulnerable about it. I don't want to do the same to my son.'

Maria was unfortunate in her feelings of isolation. Other new mothers seemed unsupportive to her and just reinforced her feelings of 'failure'. No-one such as the health visitor was sufficiently aware of her situation; otherwise, she might have been advised to become involved with a support group for women suffering from post-natal depression.

Sick mothers

It is particularly hard for girls to develop a strong sense of self-worth if one parent, and especially the mother, suffers from mental illness. Therapist Jill Curtis stresses:

'Mental health in parents is so vital to a child's healthy development.'

There has been plenty of research showing that children whose parents suffered from some psychiatric disorder are more at risk themselves of becoming mentally ill. A recent piece of original research (by Andrews, Brown and Creasey) studied the links between psychiatric disorders experienced in mothers and daughters, and the role of the quality of parenting in any link between the two.[12]

Psychiatric disorders in daughters (usually depression but some eating disorders too) were only associated with disorders in mothers when the mother's illness had been chronic or recurrent. In such cases, it was also more likely for the daughters to report 'adverse family experiences' – that is, inadequate parenting, antipathy with the mother, and physical and sexual abuse. Both poor mothering and poor fathering were likely to occur when the mother had had a chronic or recurrent disorder. Daughters who had experienced: '. . . antipathy, abuse or neglect by parents were more likely to have suffered an episode of disorder regardless of their mothers' psychiatric state.'

Mary was in her late thirties when she decided to have some therapy. She had seen friends helped by this, and though she wasn't exactly depressed, her life felt very empty, very 'grey'. Through therapy, she realised that all her life she had been coping with her mother's manic depression by trying not to feel too strongly about anything. It was, explained her therapist, as if she was driving a car with *two* brakes. She had cut out all intense feelings without realising. She put a curb on everything. She was so frightened to acknowledge the horrors of life with her mother, the times she went into psychiatric hospitals. She was clearly terrified she herself might suffer the same fate. It also became clear in therapy that Mary had chosen a boyfriend who kept a tight rein on her, reinforcing her own feelings and actions.

No wonder Mary's life felt so grey. She was experiencing

depression without realising it, suppressing any powerful feelings for fear they might take her over. She was afraid of losing control, as her mother had done through illness.

> Gillian is forty-five. Her mother was ill for many years: 'Looking back at my childhood, my mother was a rather shadowy figure. Dad got us up for school in the morning, and cooked us breakfast. I don't have very strong memories of her. When she died I felt very guilty because I was only too aware that I had never loved her as much as I had my father.' Feeling guilty about this added to Gillian's misery and depression. If she could have talked about this, with a friend or a therapist, she would have learned that such emotions are not unusual – people often prefer one parent over another – and then she could have laid her guilt to rest.

Experiencing neglect and abandonment

Losing your mother through death is obviously one of life's most painful experiences, especially if it happens in childhood or adolescence, but many women who have experienced this do at least have good memories of good mothering. However, some women have never felt wanted or loved by their mothers, and so grow up handicapped, almost bound to experience depression.

A woman who feels emotionally or physically abandoned by her mother may, as Hope Edelman explains in *Motherless Daughters*: '. . . feel like a member of the emotional underclass . . . she often develops a sense of degradation and unworthiness even more profound than that of the daughter whose mother has died.'[13] She may also feel it is all her fault.

Anna's Story

> Anna is twenty-seven: 'No-one seems to realise how much love and support you need as a child, and if you don't get this,

how easily your self-esteem can be damaged.' Anna has always known that her mother didn't want her and didn't like her, let alone love her. She is an ex-dancer, dark, intense, very pretty with a sharp intelligence. Over two years ago, she went to her family doctor for help because she had a serious phobia about the dark. Her doctor referred her to a counsellor attached to the medical centre. Within minutes, Anna found herself in tears, sobbing uncontrollably: 'The counsellor realised how depressed I was. I told her I had suicidal feelings most days, I thought this was normal. She of course knew it wasn't and referred me to regular psychotherapy. I really was quite disturbed. I had always known I didn't like my mother, and in therapy, it became clear my relationship with her was the main cause of my problems.'

Anna's father left her mother when she was pregnant. When Anna was born, she and her mother went to live with her grandmother, her mother's mother. The two women disliked each other intensely. Anna's grandfather had left home when her mother was only seven. Her grandmother always blamed her mother for driving him away. So Anna grew up, the single child of a single child, in a loveless household where men were despised and hated.

Anna's father had moved to another country: 'He didn't want to know. He didn't ever want to meet me. Early on my mother told me she didn't like me and that she didn't like children. She had never wanted me. She also instilled in me that I was not a very likeable person. She'd say I was bossy, big-mouthed, too big for my boots.'

Looking back, Anna admits she probably wasn't very nice as a child. If she is right, this is not very surprising, given the lack of good role models, of good parenting.

Anna remembers: 'My mother was very domineering. She believed that the way to discipline me was to frighten me. She was a very strict disciplinarian. She would have terrible tantrums. She was thoroughly miserable and bitter about life.

My grandmother didn't do anything about this. She just sat there most of the time being shouted at by my mother.

'I was a very frightened child, very miserable and, true, not very nice. I was very lonely and I didn't have any friends. When I went to school I quickly discovered that you won't get very far if you constantly use sarcasm as a form of communication. That's how my mother had dealt with me, and I'd picked it up from her. I just wasn't very normal, and became even more introverted as I got older.'

At sixteen, Anna left home and moved to London, to go to college: 'Then I made masses of friends. I deliberately set out to create a family of my own. I also developed a strong persona to protect myself – I was pretty, talented, fairly successful. It was my only chance of survival.'

But the early traumas had taken their toll. She realises now that she was always depressed, always thinking about suicide: 'I had no idea I was so disturbed, I thought it was all quite normal. I used to cry a lot, and drink too much, until sometimes I became hysterical. Though I had good, close friends, I felt distanced from them because of my mother. Try telling people you don't like your mother and you don't remember anything good about your childhood. The standard reply is, "It can't have been that bad." So I just stopped talking about it.'

In therapy, Anna has been able to talk freely, and to confront all her fears and anxieties: 'It took six months before I felt there was much change, when I realised the difference between talking and feeling. My therapist was tough with me, forcing me to look at myself, to confront the true me. Only then can you be true to yourself. But it was hard because as a child I had been so dominated by my mother and I had suppressed my own desires.'

Anna learned through her therapist that she was holding on to a mass of painful memories and that she had never developed the mechanism to cope with that pain, to place it in the past. She would just get very angry or very drunk; she couldn't hold or control her feelings.

Anna realises that she still needs more therapy: 'I rarely even now feel good about myself, and I think underneath everyone hates me. I could never talk about this with my mother, though I expect she realises.' Anna still visits her mother: 'I feel compelled to see her, to do what she says. I couldn't ever oppose her or argue with her. As a child, I had nobody else. I've always been aware that I hated my mother. But I found it much more difficult to admit that I would like love from her.'

Anna grew up without love and without security. Her mother instilled in her a great fear of poverty. She has a good job in management but constantly worries she will lose it.

Maggie's story

Some fifteen years older than Anna, Maggie had plenty of material security as a child, but not much love. When asked about when she first recalled feeling depressed, she replied half-jokingly that she was suicidal from an early age in a very childish way.

'I remember, like an old snapshot, our house was on a bend in the road and I would be at the top of the drive, thinking about taking my foot off the ground and rolling into the road on my scooter ... Then they'll be sorry, I thought, they don't care, but they will if I die.'

Maggie feels it was probably a little over-dramatic to call this a suicidal wish but the memory of these feelings, and their origin, is vivid years later: 'I felt unloved. Definitely unloved by my mother, always, but I can't quite remember about my father. He wasn't around enough to mitigate the feelings engendered by my mother. He got up after I'd left for school, he didn't participate much in our lives. I didn't think he didn't love me, but he was close in a distant sort of way. I do remember he was warm and cuddly. I don't ever remember my mother cuddling me. Today she can just about manage a cool peck on my cheek as a greeting.'

At forty-two, Maggie is tall, dark, warm, affectionate, but shy socially. When she was in the throes of marriage breakdown, she tried therapy but hated it. She realises now that it was probably too painful then, too close to the bone. But since then, she has done plenty of self-exploration and understands only too clearly the effects of her emotionally impoverished relationship with her mother.

Maggie is really afraid of rejection, and often simply won't risk it: 'I don't make friends easily and I know I can be quite offputting to other people. I can withdraw if I think someone likes me because I'm scared they'll change their view when they get to know me and that's another rejection.' She felt rejected by her mother from the beginning: 'I had a nanny from day one, with a starched collar, and she was wonderful. I remember feeling very sad when she left.' I have lots of theories about my childhood, I've tried to work it out. When my mother got married, she stopped work as so many women did in those days. But she was completely uneducated and had no interests except shopping. I think she saw children as just another fashion accessory, she didn't want to spend any time with us.

'She has often told me what a terrible experience my birth was, and how she tried to breast-feed me and couldn't. So there was obviously a problem with bonding, and maybe I always reminded her of failure. I also remember my grandmother blaming me for my mother's ulcers. It was all my fault because I'd upset her. But she went into a clinic from time to time for these ulcers and now with hindsight and a bit of knowledge, I wonder if the ulcers were all a front and I suspect my mother was having a complete mental breakdown.'

Not surprisingly, Maggie left home and went off to university without a moment's sadness at leaving. She never went back to live at home, and she rarely sees her mother. Her intelligence and resourcefulness prevented her having a breakdown like her mother's. But she has suffered several bouts of depression, mainly linked to relationship problems, and she recognises the patterns and the negative thinking passed down from her mother. She is now working hard to bring up her own children differently.

It is difficult for Maggie and other women with similar upbringings not to feel bitter and angry with their mothers. But Maggie also accepts that her mother suffered, to some extent, from the social mores of the time. Women like her were not expected to work once they were married. People did not question the idea that only marriage and childbearing could bring fulfilment to a woman. So if she didn't find this to be the case, she was bound to feel abnormal and depressed. In different ways, the sadnesses and frustrations of so many women have been passed down through the generations. It is that potent mix of early conditioning and childhood experiences, later mitigated or not in adulthood, which creates our self and, most importantly, our perception of that self.

Learning Points

✔ Girls are still brought up differently from boys, from an early age, and this can harm our self-esteem.

✔ We are brought up to please, to be attractive, to be nice and sweet, passive, helpless.

✔ We are encouraged to care for and nurture others. We do this well, but society doesn't value such activities.

✔ We are conditioned to feel guilty from an early age, and it's usually inappropriate guilt.

✔ Our mother's love and approval are crucial for the development of our self-esteem and sense of self-worth, not only during our childhood but throughout our adult life.

3 Women in Society Today – Still the Outsiders?

I have explained how important self-esteem is for good mental health. Many women have low self-esteem and therefore many women suffer from depression. We feel powerless, out of control – or, rather, not in control – of our lives.

This isn't just because of our early childhood experience and social conditioning; it is also a very real consequence of the inequalities we suffer every day as women in our society. These inequalities are still huge – at work, at home, and financially. We struggle to care for our families as well as working outside the home. There is poor childcare provision, and we are usually the ones who care for elderly parents and relatives, often with little outside support or financial help. If society and, therefore, men don't value women's contribution, how easy is it for us to value ourselves?

I went to University in the 1960s, along with many of my friends. Volumes have been written about the excitement of the times, the freedom, the drugs and the rock 'n roll. But what was also exciting for many young women like me was that we felt the world was our oyster. I had been brought up, and this wasn't always common, to believe I could do anything as long as I worked hard and received a good education. I hadn't experienced sexist attitudes at home or at school. Far from it: my younger brother and I shared washing dishes and such-like; my parents always encouraged me to go to university and follow a career; my schoolteachers did the same.

It was only when we entered the real world, of work, of relationships, of marriage, that we realised it was so much a man's world. Women who chose to stay at home with young children were looked down on by many including, I have to say, their 'sisters' in careers. Their husbands (most people married then) did very little in the house or with the children; I am of that generation that thanks a partner, or used to, for doing the dishes! Many women of my generation chose between marriage and children, and careers. For example, in the field of television only thirty per cent of the women in 'creative' jobs have children, a far lower proportion than among the men.

Those women of my generation who opted for both family and career, struggled to find any time for themselves. When they took time out to care for young children, their careers suffered. When they divorced, they often lost out financially.

It's still a man's world

It is not so very different today, even though women in their twenties and, to some extent, thirties expect more, and rightly so. Over the past twenty-five years, there have been legal reforms as well as many more advances in education, attitudes to women working, and contraception. Many of us live happily on our own and lead interesting, independent lives. Others negotiate different forms of partnership from their parents'. But still there is discrimination at work, inequalities in marriage, insufficient childcare, and financial inequalities exacerbated by the fact that women live longer. Most of us work because we have to – one wage or salary isn't enough for a basic standard of living, let alone any luxuries.

There is, too, the double standard. The Prince of Wales can get away with having an adulterous affair with a married woman. He probably gains 'Brownie points' from the lads for behaving like this. But his wife Diana is constantly harried by the press for possible relationships with married men, and criticised for her dress sense and her mothering style.

Single mothers are criticised for fecklessness and easy sexual behaviour. They are accused of deliberately getting pregnant to claim social security and a council house. Fathers may be chased for money by the Child Support Agency, but this has caused an outcry among men. It's also true to say that men aren't castigated by society in the same way as women for marital breakdown. All the Government's calls for a return to 'family values' have succeeded only in laying more responsibilities and burdens on women. It is as if parenting is still seen as solely our responsibility. No wonder there are high levels of depression among those of us who are single mothers.

Kate Figes is a woman in her early thirties, the daughter of feminist writer Eva Figes who wrote powerful polemics in the 1960s and 70s. Now, in 1995, writing about the birth of her own daughter in *Because of Her Sex*[1] Kate writes: 'I knew already that she was destined to struggle harder than any man if she was to succeed in her chosen field, that she was likely to plummet to the depths of depression, anger and disappointment and soar occasionally to the heights of rapture and passion.'

Having it all

Women form fifty-one per cent of the population of the UK. We are told endlessly by the media that we are living in the post-feminist era – we don't need feminism, all the battles are won. But let's look at the 1995 report from the Central Statistical Office, *Social Focus on Women*.[2] The Introduction implies women are in control, moving onwards and ever upwards: 'The traditional distinction between the woman's role of homemaker and the man's role of breadwinner has been eroded. Modern family planning methods have made it far easier for women to take control of the planning of their own lives as they can now choose the timing and spacing of their children and limit the number of children they have . . .'

But first let's take a look at the cover. It shows an elegantly dressed, immaculately made-up and coiffed woman, carrying briefcase and baby. So we've made it, but at what cost? This is the stuff of fantasy. If we turn to the statistics and commentaries, we realise how far we still have to go to achieve equality. It's true that more women are working outside the home, but in low paid, part-time employment. So much for the view (wrongly held) that we monstrous regiment of women have stolen the lucrative jobs from men. We need to face up to reality: many industries and professions still discriminate against women; and women who go out to work still do most of the housework as well as caring for children and elderly relatives.

As *The Guardian* leader commented when the report appeared: 'Now we have a reference work which highlights how the pace of change has outstripped the structures which order work, family life and children. The result? Ask any working mother: she's knackered.'[3]

In the thirty-five to forty-five age group, the key years of childrearing, more than seventy per cent of women are in paid employment. But we still do far more housework and childcare, even if we work full-time. So much for the 'new man'. Women tend to prepare the evening meal, do the washing and ironing and the household cleaning, while men tend to be responsible for repairs to household equipment. At least we've made strides in some areas:

- Household shopping is equally shared in nearly fifty per cent of couples.

- Men are more involved in household tasks than they were over ten years ago.

- Men who do the evening dishes increased from seventeen per cent in 1981 to twenty-eight per cent in 1991.

However, despite these advances, women's free time has fallen by ten per cent since the mid 1980s.

This report is just part of the massive body of evidence which shows that women are still perceived as inferior; many individual men may not feel this, but the perception is institutionalised in society. Why otherwise don't we receive equal pay? Why aren't there as many female bosses at boardroom level? All these factors contribute to our feelings, if not of inferiority, then of lower self-esteem and self-confidence than many men. We feel powerless, at home and at work. We also feel exhausted much of the time, trying to run a home and a career. The inevitable consequence is depression. We shouldn't feel depressed about this unfair burden, we should feel angry – and show it. Why should women do so much more in the home than men? It is quite healthy to feel down when you're tired and fraught, at the end of your tether trying to fit thirty hours into twenty-four.

Facing reality

There will be little change until we all, and especially politicians and policy makers, recognise certain key facts:

* Most women have children, and want part-time work so that they can care for their children.

* Most fathers do not seem over-keen to take on the practical task of looking after their offspring.

* Women who take career breaks to look after children almost always suffer in comparison with their male colleagues.

* Very few women have flexible working arrangements.

* Part-time work is low paid and insecure, contributing to women's feelings of powerlessness, especially if they are single parents.

Family structure is changing, and no government can stop this. Divorce is on the increase and many couples choose not to marry. One of the effects of this is an increase in the financial instability of women and their children. After separation or divorce, for example, nearly half of women see their income fall, compared with a fifth of men in the same situation.

It is not surprising that women are delaying the decision to start a family. Many of us wish to achieve more in career terms before taking a career break. More women than ever are not having children at all, and research shows the percentage of childless women is likely to increase. One can only speculate on the reasons, but I believe it is partly to do with the lower status applied to women with children, and the difficulties, both practical and financial, of combining work with family life.

There are many siren calls about the collapse of community, of society as we used to know it. Women are criticised for this, for wanting both work and children, for demanding equal status. But the strong warp and weft of society depends hugely on women's contributions. We are the ones who place particular value on relationships. We are the ones who stress the importance of communicating with each other, of caring and nurturing, whether it be for tiny children or elderly parents with Alzheimer's Disease.

- In six out of ten couples, it is the mother who is responsible for looking after a sick child.

- Over one in ten women are caring for a parent or parent-in-law.

- One in twenty women are looking after a friend or neighbour.

The Guardian leader in response to *Social Focus on Women* was powerful on this issue, arguing that women: '. . . should not be penalised or discriminated against in the workplace for making the well-being of their children and consideration for their relationships with partners, friends and extended families a priority.'[4] Furthermore, it continues: 'Ending discrimination in the workplace is not only a question of rights. It is about mobilising skills in which we are told women are particularly adept, such as human relations and communications; it is a matter of sound common sense . . . The double burden of competing at work whilst maintaining women's traditional priority of human relationships is punishing.' Once again, feeling depressed because of discrimination at work and dealing with the home is quite normal. Superwoman doesn't, and never did, exist. But women are too good at coping with a whole range of activities; we can focus on more than one thing at a time, writing a report and listening out for a baby's cries, for example. But this ability can add to our burden.

What have we achieved?

Women today are more likely than their mothers' generation to hold some form of educational qualification. The unemployment rate of women with no educational qualifications is almost four times that of women educated to above 'A' level standard (although this may be partly due to the unqualified women being older).

There has recently been much attention paid in the media to the fact that girls are doing so much better than boys academically.

• In 1994, not only did girls beat boys at GCSE but they also had more top grades in science, a traditionally male subject.

A report by Keele University's Centre for Successful Schools said that girls: '. . . are consistently more positive, better motivated, better at getting on with their teachers and better behaved.'5 Yet girls and boys don't realise this (the classic female lack of confidence in operation again). The report continues to explain that: '. . . on the question which asks the pupils to assess their own abilities, the answers reveal that more boys than girls think they are able or very able, and fewer boys than girls think they are below average.

Yet the actual results at GCSE show these perceptions to be the reverse of the truth.'

Girls read more, other studies show, and have better verbal skills than boys. Girls are emerging better qualified than boys for the new jobs, for example, in the language-based service sector. The numbers going to university are now virtually equal between boys and girls, but it's noticeable that girls are not always being encouraged to apply to the centres of excellence, such as Oxford and Cambridge.

These changes are partly the result of the Equal Opportunities Policy operating in all schools, whether state or private. But rather than celebrating the achievements of these girls, many commentators tend to depict it as a disaster for men. It's the old fear of women emasculating men. The horrifying implication is that the future may be female and men will be thrown on the rubbish heap.

Where are the jobs?

We are producing an increasingly well-educated number of young women, but they still don't have the same job opportunities as their male counterparts. And when the time comes to have children, those opportunities become even more limited. As the MP Clare Short commented: 'We've got a rifle range in the House of Commons and no creche.' Nor do many large companies offer creches and other childcare facilities to female employees. It is still up to us to organise often complicated and tiresome combinations of childcare.

Women seem to be immensely committed to working and are gaining better and better qualifications. We are well represented in medicine and law, for example, and though the majority of us are in part-time jobs, the numbers in full-time work are rising, whereas the number of men is decreasing. But we are fighting a rearguard battle. There are still very few women in top positions in any field and this is partly because organisations and companies have failed, and/or refuse, to accommodate themselves to women who work and have children. We all suffer from a culture which demands employees to be in the office all the time, and many of us feel lucky to have a job at all. There is also the new problem of 'presenteeism' whereby people stay in the office longer than they need in order to impress their boss. Busy women with children at home and a partner who contributes little in practical terms, cannot possibly fit in with this.

Not only do many talented and well-qualified women fail to do as well as they could because they choose motherhood, but the country is also wasting a huge amount of untapped expertise – not to mention the money spent on educating and training these women. Setting aside the question of equality, it doesn't make economic sense, nor does it help relations between the two sexes. We begrudge having to do more than our fair share, while men feel bitter about missing out on parenting. There is, of course, the social cost of separation and divorce to contend with too.

According to a recent article by Sarah Hogg in *The Daily Telegraph*[6]:

- Women still occupy only about one managerial post in ten in Britain's public companies.

- Women account for less than ten per cent of the top civil service grades.

- About seven per cent of appointments to the judiciary and less than ten per cent of the seats in the House of Commons are held by women.

- Trade union management is still male-dominated.

It suits companies to keep women in part-time, insecure work, but this means that many of us remain dependent on our male partners to earn more. We also have far less access to training and promotion if we work part-time. We have to rely on low paid, flexible work because we cannot afford expensive, full-time childcare, and state funded care isn't available. Economic liberalisation and the dominance of the market mean that those with the least earning power, i.e. women with children, suffer most. Even when we do have full-time work and careers, we are often less well paid because we choose those areas of work which are traditonally female and therefore traditionally have lower rates of pay – nursing, teaching, secretarial work.

In many areas of work, women still haven't attained equal pay with their male colleagues; this is true in both manual and non-manual work. Britain foots most European tables of pay differentials:

- According to a 1993 report, The Gender Pay Gap: Some European Comparisons by Jill Rubery, the gross monthly earnings of non-manual women workers in Britain average just fifty-four per cent of men's, as compared with sixty-six per cent in France and nearly seventy per cent in Germany.[7]

Poverty

Many women are significantly poorer than men, partly because we often receive lower pay, but also because of personal circumstances such as divorce, caring for young children or looking after elderly relatives.

- In 1992, one half of all full-time working women earned

below two thirds of the average weekly male wage, with women from ethnic groups frequently being paid even less.

After separation and divorce, women tend to become much poorer than their ex-partners. Many women, especially single mothers and elderly women, are living on non-contributory state benefits, such as Income Support. Many women too, find they are not eligible for unemployment benefit or a full pension because they have taken breaks from employment. In fact, most of the country's poor are women and their children.

- In 1988, the number of women living in poverty (defined as income below fifty per cent of the UK average after housing costs) was 5.8 million, compared with 2.2 million in 1979.

Elderly women feature among this country's poorest.

- In 1991, only fifteen per cent of female pensioners were entitled to a full state pension.

Many of today's divorcees will be poor when they reach retirement age; it is only very recently that divorced wives have won the right to half their ex-husband's occupational pension for the period of the marriage.

Health problems

Women living on low incomes will always put their own needs last. They will eat less, and less well, than the rest of the family. This has long-term consequences for their health since poor diet certainly contributes to the development of heart disease and other health problems. Not surprisingly, women from middle-class, more affluent homes have healthier diets than women from manual, less affluent households.

- The 1995 report *Social Focus on Women* states that underweight women are more at risk of osteoporosis and hip fractures.[8]

There is plenty of evidence that poverty is a major factor in creating health problems among women and men. Stress creates ill health, and poverty obviously exacerbates stress. But many women, not necessarily poor, suffer from stress because of the huge pressures on them from work and home. Recent research included in the 1993 Health Survey for England, conducted by the Office of Population Censuses and Surveys, revealed some disturbing trends[9]:

- About fifteen per cent of women interviewed reported that they had experienced quite a lot, or a great deal, of stress in the four weeks before the interview.

- Nearly a quarter of women who smoked twenty or more cigarettes a day reported high levels of stress.

- Although the numbers of women smoking have dropped over the past years, men are more likely to give up smoking than women.

- Smoking is especially common among younger women and women in manual households.

- The proportion of women aged eighteen and over drinking over the sensible level has increased from nine per cent in 1984 to eleven per cent in 1992–3.

- Young women, single women and widows are more likely to be heavy drinkers.

Violence against women

Another major factor affecting women's self-esteem and wellbeing is the violence in our society: Domestic violence is widespread, though it seems that violent, even murderous husbands may receive more lenient sentences than wives who have killed their abusing husbands. Women suffer rape (two thirds committed by men they know), sexual and physical abuse, especially as children, and sexual harassment, often at work.

- A report from the International Labour Organisation in August 1995, stated that up to thirty per cent of women in industrialised countries are subjected to frequent, serious, sexual harrassment at work.[10]

Women who live with violent men may feel trapped and helpless, especially if they are financially dependent on the men. Women tend to blame themselves if they are raped, or battered by their partners. They feel worthless and powerless, and depression is frequently the result. Their feelings may be exacerbated by far from sympathetic treatment from the police, the health and social services, even their own families. The misconceived views that 'she asked for it' and 'a woman who says No means Yes' die hard.

Barrister Helena Kennedy makes an interesting point in her book *Eve Was Framed: Women and British Justice*: 'For the most part I just accepted that there were higher expectations of women . . . Men were simply victims of their own appetites, hardly capable of free will when it came to sex or violence, and it was up to us to act as the restraining influence. After all, woman was responsible for the original sin. It was only later that I came to the conclusion that Eve had been framed.'

The other problem for all women is that fear can become an integral part of our lives, because we know we are vulnerable to male violence, at home and on the streets. Our fears are often greater than the reality of the statistics, but if we know someone who has been raped or been mugged, it's hard not to feel frightened ourselves. That fear adds to our general feelings of powerlessness and lack of control in our lives.

An equal society is a healthy society

It should be obvious that both men and women will benefit from a more equal society, and from greater value being placed on women's contribution to society. Interestingly, in the world of development issues, the word 'gender' has replaced the word 'women'. Nikki van der Gaag explains in a recent article for the *New Internationalist* that this is based on: '. . . the understanding that just working on women's situations is not going to make a difference, whereas working with men and women is.' She explains that men are no longer seen as the enemy: '. . . although male structures and patriarchal thinking are still the major agents of repression . . . It is less threatening to male-led governments to consider 'women' as a separate category than to acknowledge that it is the relationship between men and women that is crucial . . . the only way to bring men on board is to show that change is in their interest.'[11]

In a time of major social changes, of terrible poverty, of changing working conditions which adversely affect both women and men and dehumanise their lives, it seems crazy for the two not to be more in tune with each other.

The world of work

Research has shown that paid work can protect women against depression, and not just as a source of income. It offers us social contacts, may alleviate boredom and so raises our self-esteem. As I explained earlier, though, for too many of us this does not apply because we may find ourselves in low paid, stress creating, unrewarding work.

I spoke to some women specifically about how work affects them, and can increase or decrease their self-esteem. Many women spoke of the importance of their work and how, in comparison with other aspects of their lives, it gave them confidence.

> Sheila is a senior manager in the NHS. She admits to feeling depressed quite often because of her marriage, which is unsatisfying in so many ways. But when things go wrong at work, she becomes angry rather than miserable: 'I'm forty-two and I was brought up to think I could do anything as far as careers were concerned. I have a high level of commitment to my work, which I often enjoy, despite very long hours. That gives me a high level of self-worth.'

> At forty-five, Gina is divorced with two teenage children. Out of financial necessity, she was forced to do more training and now has a demanding managerial post: 'Work has provided such a focus for my life, especially through the ghastly years of separation and divorce. I just don't know what I'd do if I lost my job. Working gives me a sense of confidence, which I don't feel about my personal life. It gives me a sense of belonging, of security, I suppose. I'm quite shy so I find work easier to deal with than many social situations.'

*   *   *

Both these women took 'time out' from work to bring up young children. Gina particularly suffered from this; she is older than most of the other (male) managers, and will not have a good pension. But other women regret the fact that they put work first and have missed out on having children, and sometimes a good relationship. As one very successful, divorced, childless woman said to me: 'A good job doesn't keep you warm at night.'

We shouldn't have to make such choices – few men do – but things are unlikely to improve given the increasingly insecure nature of work and the increase in part-time and self-employed work. This is hitting women at every age. Competition at work and job insecurity are very real causes of depression because they hit our self-esteem which is often already fragile around work issues.

Unemployment

Unemployment is, not surprisingly, hard for women, but particularly for those of us who are single. If we are living on a very low income, we can feel even more isolated because we are unable to afford to take part in social activities with friends.

Joanna is thirty-one, a pretty, intelligent computer analyst who has been out of work for several months. This reflects the competitive world in which she works rather than her own abilities. Intellectually, she knows this but she experiences some days of rock-bottom depression, as well as anxiety about her financial position: 'Sometimes I just feel like I've climbed down into the coalshed for two days. Then the sun shines and I feel better for a while. It's also very exhausting. You can feel yourself mentally and physically hauling yourself out of the coalshed. No-one else can do it for you. I feel I have so little control of the situation. After several years of on-off freelance work, I feel ground down and my confidence is so much lower than ten years ago when I started out. I was probably too cocky then.

'Being unemployed makes me feel my automatic membership of normal society has lapsed, because we are all to some extent defined by what work we do. My pride is hurt too, I had expectations and ambitions. I work hard. It doesn't seem to make any difference. It's devastating socially too. People would rather you lied and said you were working. You know you've made them feel uncomfortable.

'It's always on your mind. You have to try to get back that belief in yourself, however many rejections you receive. You run yourself down. You have to start shovelling back the bits of self-esteem lying around you. But it feels like an amputation. I'm ready to do a job, a good job, one I'm trained for, but I can't. I'm worried my brain's withering away.'

These feelings are not, of course, experienced only by women who are out of work. Men in the same position suffer in the same way. But unemployment or sacking does add to women's already fragile self-esteem.

Maggie was made redundant at almost the same time as her divorce was finalised. Two major life events in one month! She had been expecting the sack for months as many people in her firm had already been made redundant or sacked: 'It had also become a ghastly place to work and I had been looking round for other jobs. When I was told, I felt weirdly calm, went off to the dentist, and then returned to clear my desk. I didn't feel totally unempowered. I had seen it happen to other people, men as well as women. In fact several of us had lots of champagne that evening, it was fun.

'Friends and ex-colleagues were also very supportive, ringing up to see how I was getting along, and making suggestions about work. I always remember the people who said nice things. Now I know when something happens like a death or redundancy, it's good to ring up. Don't be afraid of saying the wrong thing.'

Maggie also knows that she should have been more active in finding work when the redundancies began some months earlier, but like many women, and as in other areas of her life, she was passive, waiting for something to be done to her.

Diana who worked in banking, was made redundant and offered redundancy counselling. She was very sceptical at first, but decided to try it: 'I thought the practical stuff was useful, advice on writing CVs, job interviews, that sort of thing. But I was deeply sceptical about the psychological testing. So when I did it I was staggered. They had captured "me" and gave me insights into my character I hadn't possessed before. This helped me rethink strategies in the office and then helped me decide on what area of work to tackle next.' Within four months, she had a new job.

Being made redundant and being unemployed are very depressing experiences, and doing something to change this is not always easy. It isn't always in our control, especially when unemployment is so high. But we can try to be positive and see the time of redundancy and unemployment as one for re-evaluating what we want out of life and, perhaps, reordering our priorities. Again, our financial circumstances will dictate how easily we can do this. Women with solvent and supportive partners, or who have considerable redundancy payments, will be in a better position to reconsider their career, perhaps pursuing a course of higher education or a major career change. But for any of us in this position, feeling bad will be better if we *use* the feelings once again, look hard at what is causing the depression and then deal with it in as practical and positive a way as possible. That was clearly the experience of Maggie and Diana.

Learning Points

If your depression is linked with work:

- ✔ If you're unemployed, you will feel low and lacking in self-confidence. This is normal as our status and wellbeing are closely linked with work.
- ✔ If you're constantly exhausted because you're combining work and looking after a family, it is time to look hard at your life and try to simplify it. Make sure your partner and your children do their fair share of household tasks. It is not up to you to do everything.
- ✔ If your job is insecure, don't wait passively to receive your redundancy notice. Take the initiative and start looking out for new opportunities.
- ✔ If you can't find the job you want, it is never too late to acquire extra qualifications and further education. You may even be able to get a grant for studying.

4   The Importance of Relationships

Ask most women what caused their depression, and they will answer 'relationships', usually meaning relationships with men – boyfriends, lovers, husbands, ex-partners. Psychologist Bernice Andrews, who has done considerable research into women, depression and low self-esteem, agrees: 'What makes women depressed is men, and their relationships with them. Men still have the upper hand.'

The gay women I interviewed also said that their depression usually sprang from problems with a relationship. It is the desire for closeness and intimacy, including sex, which makes us so vulnerable.

Writing about relationships is rather like confronting a tangled ball of wool, trying to pull out individual strands and finding others twisted around them. Women will spend hours, days, months, agonising on their own, or with friends, about relationships. We need to accept the importance of these attachments, and try to understand why we become so downcast when they seem to fail. Only then can we cope better in the future, hopefully by avoiding the repetition of unhealthy patterns but also by recognising why we feel as we do.

I'm not going to take a 'life stages' approach because although some aspects of relationships are in the spotlight at certain ages, life is generally much more flexible now. Take, for example, a group of women in their late thirties.

- A has been married for fourteen years and has two teenage children.

- B has been married for four years and has a two-year-old.

- C is divorced after fifteen years and has three children.

- D is having a long affair with a married man, and is wondering about the chances of motherhood.

- E is planning to marry a divorced man and contemplating late motherhood.

It isn't just about ages and stages of maturity. It is also about the universals of loss, separation, intimacy, solitude.

Fears and anger

As I have explained in earlier chapters, a poor marriage will cause depression for many reasons, whether these are conscious or not. When a relationship doesn't work, we feel a failure, and we may also remember other 'failures', such as not being 'good enough' for our parents. We may experience an overwhelming sense of inadequacy, looking back over a past which, in the darkest times, seems littered with disasters.

We become depressed because we are literally suppressing, pushing down, strong feelings we do not want to confront, or cannot cope with. This may be because we have been conditioned to feel that any strong emotions are 'bad'.

Mary was like this. Every time it would have been appropriate to feel excited, just before a holiday, for instance, she would become crippled by anxiety and depression. She would just take to her bed. She didn't feel able to learn to drive because that would be exciting. Somehow, through her childhood, in the midst of a very volatile family, she had learned to suppress her feelings and her natural sense of adventure.

We are also afraid of loneliness, lack of status, and poverty. Depression is frequently caused by loss, and every relationship risks loss – whether through separation and divorce (if we are married) or, ultimately, through death. Many women feel depressed because they do not have a relationship with a man, they do not have the 'someone special' that almost every woman craves.

Our early childhood experiences of relationships are vital in forming the bedrock on which we later build relationships as adults. Obviously it is harder to form good adult relationships if our parents were not, or did not seem to be, happy in their own relationship. Children of divorced parents are more likely themselves to experience divorce. Children whose parent, or parents, died when they were young will not have the role models necessary to help them forge a successful long-term relationship as adults. If our basic emotional needs are not met in childhood, because of death or abandonment, or because our parents, especially our mothers, are unable or unwilling to meet our needs, then we are at more risk of experiencing poor relationships as adults.

Obviously early experiences influence our choice of partner. It is a cliché, but nevertheless true, that we often marry a 'parent', and not always the parent we were closest to. Fatherless women may find themselves searching for the classic father figure, whatever their own father was like.

The 'bad boy'

Many of us know the lure of the 'bad boy', the wholly unsuitable character, of whom the American novelist Erica

Jong writes so eloquently in *Fear of Fifty*.[1] She believes that women so often fall for 'bad boys' (and she cites some famous examples of women writers, artists, and fierce feminists) because they help us break our bonds with home and mother: 'Passion is a great catalyst for growing up . . . Nice women are drawn to rule-breaking men because our female-goodness training is so absolute that we deeply need to find the suppressed part of ourselves: rebellion. We can't always break free alone, we need a man to cut the ribbon with – if not for – us. What ribbon? The blood-red ribbon that still binds us to our mothers and fathers.'

Perhaps every woman should experience an affair with the 'bad boy'. As Jong writes, for a woman: 'Loving a bad boy means loving the bad boy in herself, asserting her freedom, the wildness of her soul. The bad boy is the rebel part of herself that her female upbringing has usually tried to quash.'

If we meet the 'bad boy' early in our adult lives and release that part of ourselves, then we have more chance of resolving those contradictions and conflicts within ourselves, and discovering our true 'self'. Then we can perhaps decide on a more 'mature', healthier relationship. Unfortunately, for many women, the 'bad boy' never comes along, or arrives at the wrong time, that is, when they are married to their so-called Prince Charming.

Myth and reality

As young girls, we have all read the fairy stories in which the hero and heroine marry and live happily ever after. Marriage is indeed a very powerful myth, which the American writer Carolyn S. Heilbrun has accused of being 'the most persistent of myths imprisoning women'.[2] American researcher

Dana Crowley Jack explains in *Silencing the Self*: 'As a myth, it promises intimacy, identity, and a well-marked life path that even young children know by heart'.[3] What the fairy tales don't tell us is that taking this conventional path too often reinforces our lack of self-esteem, or reduces it, and takes away our sense of 'self'. We have been 'taught' to put the man centre stage; he is the hero of the play we call Marriage. Couples are constantly trying to change this, to make their relationships more equal, but as we've already seen, role reversal is still unusual and sharing tasks is by no means universal.

The poet Milton was writing *Paradise Lost* over 300 years ago but his thoughts on Adam and Eve still permeate our culture:

> For contemplation he and valour formed;
> For softness she and sweet attractive grace,
> He for God only, she for God in him . . .'

Psychotherapist Jill Curtis sees many depressed women who have suppressed their energies and ambitions because of their partners' wishes: 'They so often say, "I couldn't do that, he wouldn't like it."'

Losing your 'self'

Women who have experienced depression frequently talk about losing themselves, losing a sense of their own identity, losing their way, in relationships. Part of this is simply practical: caring for small children and a home, plus outside work, leaves precious little time for ourselves, for other interests. So many of us long for the day when we can 'write the novel' or create a beautiful garden.

After years of a reasonably happy marriage, one woman said to me: 'I feel I've been given no choices in life, no-one asked me what I'd like to have done. Life just happened.' Single women, too, and married women with children also fall into the trap of subsuming their needs in those of their man.

> Louise was a doctor, a psychiatrist who specialised in treating adolescents. But the two significant relationships in her twenties and thirties were with two men who were not so much uninterested in her work as threatened by it. Consequently, alongside her books on psychology, Louise's bookshelves carry tomes on African history and economics, and on rock 'n roll. Such subjects weren't anathema to her, but she would not necessarily have chosen them for herself. But like many women, she sees taking an interest in her man's life and work as being important in making a good relationship.

For most women over the age of thirty-five today, marriage was certainly seen as an important goal in life, whether or not they wanted a career. Too often, they 'lost' themselves in that relationship but didn't always realise why they were miserable.

Janet's story

> Janet, who is now forty-eight, married when she was twenty, like her mother before her and most of her friends: 'I just wanted to get married and have kids. My best Christmas present was my dolly and her pram, I still remember that. I first met Mike when I was seventeen; he was a friend of my brother's. But he travelled a lot so from seventeen to twenty, I stayed at home a lot waiting for him.'
>
> The romance didn't last very long: 'When my first child was eighteen months old, my husband came home with a dose of gonorrhoea. I found the clinic card in his pocket and suspected.

I managed to trick one of his friends into telling me the truth and then I told Mike to go. I realised I had been so wrapped up with my baby that I just hadn't noticed things weren't the same. We only had sex about once every six weeks. I always got up early to make Mike a sandwich lunch for work, and there was always a meal on the table at night. When he said he was going out, which was most evenings, he'd say it was a "boys only" night. It was only later I realised he'd slept with every slag he met. I met one of them in the street and what really hurt me was that she was so ugly, wearing dirty clothes, with the hem of her coat hanging down.'

A few months later, Janet was persuaded by her husband's friends to take him back. They said he was suicidal, 'a changed man'. She had a second daughter, and four years later, answered the 'phone one morning to a woman asking for Mike. She assumed he was up to his old tricks and confronted him.

'He was lying on the settee, and was drunk. "That sounds like Doris," he admitted. "What's wrong with that? You don't turn me on any more."' I must have been mad. I said, "It's her or me," and he agreed to give her up. But then something happened. I found myself thinking, "What am I doing? I don't like him any more, let alone love him." I just switched off and told him to go. I remember sitting on the floor crying with my children.'

Janet is a very practical and strong woman. Her husband gave her nothing so she struggled with the DSS and then did as many jobs as she could find. But dealing with the emotional side was more difficult.

'When we finally split, I immediately went into another relationship. It's like giving myself a pat on the back. I want someone to put me back on the pedestal, then I'll feel good again. That's the way I handled things.

'For over ten years I had various relationships. I didn't want to face what was going on in my life. I felt a failure because my marriage hadn't been like my mum and dad's. I didn't like having lots of boyfriends but I couldn't cope otherwise. I hated my own company so it was all a frantic search for someone to be with.' The search eventually led her to Steve, who had three children of his own: 'He was not my perfect, handsome man but within two weeks of our meeting, he said I was moving in and I did, with my daughters. They were horrified. Possibly it was something to do with security. But it was my usual solution, just find another man and I'll feel all right.'

The first eighteen months were 'really happy' even though Janet worked so hard, cooking supper for nine people most evenings: 'But suddenly one day he stopped being Mr Nice Guy. He said, "You're not going anywhere, you're just staying here." He became domineering and harsh. He'd hit his own children, not mine, and they would cower if he came through the door and wasn't whistling.'

Looking back, Janet doesn't understand why she didn't leave him sooner: 'I was crying all the time, I knew I couldn't go on like this, but I just didn't know what to do, and my children were so important to me. I felt I just had to get on with life, even though I know I was fed up with being the underdog. Then he had an affair with my friend, and that was it. I'd put up with so many things but this was the end. Of course he denied it but I left with my children and one suitcase, all I could carry.'

Now, several years later, Janet is happily living with a man, and her children are still close to her and in good jobs. It took a long time to arrive at the 'happy ending' but Janet admits: 'In the past I didn't want any more than what I seemed to have, a husband and children.'

The search for 'someone special'

Today's teenagers and twentysomethings may worry less about the actual ceremony of marriage, or the binding contract. But they still, like their older sisters, long for the important relationship – to live with someone special for ever and ever. When this doesn't happen, or when a relationship fails to live up to our expectations, life can seem very grey, and nothing else may matter.

At this age, often a volatile time emotionally, young women deal with feelings of emptiness and alienation by using drugs, alcohol, tobacco, and relationships.

Coline, aged twenty, recalls: 'I'd been really depressed, not eating properly, not sleeping. A good friend, who herself had experienced anorexia, suggested I saw a counsellor. He was great but then I met a new boyfriend and stopped seeing the counsellor. You see, I felt normal again. I'm with a bloke. Story of my life!'

Marian, aged twenty-one is in her second year at university studying French. Her lecturers expect her to achieve a very good degree, possibly a first, but she is deeply depressed because there's no man in her life: 'I have been depressed for over three months, since a major relationship ended. It wasn't exactly a shock, we'd been talking about splitting up, but I've been overwhelmed by my feelings since. I'm crying all the time, and want to talk about it obsessively. Everyone seems to be part of a couple except me. So I feel I'm not interesting, that I have nothing to say. On good days I know this is irrational, but it's how I feel.'

Marian wasn't so much missing her boyfriend as the experience of having a boyfriend, the pleasure and the comforts: 'We'd split up before and I knew it was right to split up. What really upset me was the loss of a friend, and of a sexual relationship. Being with him had given me a lot of confidence, made me feel sexually attractive. I no longer feel attractive. I'm much more confident with a man around.' She also admits to feeling 'on the shelf', at the great age of twenty-one: 'All my friends seem to be getting married. Women still have expectations of getting a man, a husband, children.'

Marian doesn't have a 'hazy, romantic' view of marriage, she says, mainly because her parents, who married at a young age, are divorced: 'I'm looking for security and stability, to make a home, to nest. Life is so scary, it would be nice to have a man to go through it all with.' She also laughingly admits that she would enjoy the actual day, the ceremony of a wedding: 'I want the day, the pomp and the circumstance.'

Daughter of a strong feminist and a sixties marriage, Marian is not as unusual as one might think. She just may be more honest. If we take a look at any magazine for young women, say *Company* or *Cosmopolitan*, we can see the conflicts are there still. Articles about the assertive young woman, whether assertive in the office or in bed, watching football or surfing the Internet, lie side by side with articles offering 'Eligible men; they're sexy and single and looking for love' or 'Relationships in the 90s: the magic ingredients that turn passionate affairs into permanent partnerships.' Agony columns are as popular as ever; the problems, almost wholly to do with relationships and sex, are not so different from twenty or thirty years ago, except in the frank way they're described. This mix of reading reflects the mix of interests among most young women (and older ones too, who are often to be found reading their daughters' magazines).

Every woman, at whatever age, agonises over relationships: finding one, mending one, leaving one, losing one. Not that men don't experience pain over relationships, but they seem more able to compartmentalise, to put different aspects of their lives into separate boxes. Or, once over the initial misery, they are better at cutting themselves off from their emotions, perhaps through a series of sexual flings or punishing exercise routines. In a recent article in *The Guardian*[4], a leading scientist wrote that he used jogging as an anti-depressant and, interestingly, he reckoned that most male runners were mildly depressed. A male friend, a keen runner, supported this idea, noting how many men in his running group were separated or divorced. (I am not for a minute suggesting that every man who exercises is emotionally repressed, just that men may have different coping strategies.)

Do we depend too much on relationships?

The poet Byron wrote in *Don Juan*:

> Man's love is of man's life a thing apart,
> 'Tis woman's whole existence.

Was he just reflecting the social realities of the time, when no woman worked if she did not have to, and women were seen as inferior to men. Or was he describing a universal truth? And if he was, who is the wiser, man or woman?

Relationships do seem to be more important to women; relationships with family and friends as well as with partners. American research, quoted by Ashurst and Hall in *Understanding Women in Distress*, shows that men seem to prize achievement and they also trend to put space between themselves, lest they be overtaken or put down: 'They are competitive and more able to exist on their own, caring less for the opinions of others, except in so far as they need approval in order to succeed. Women, on the other hand, need to exist in a network of family and friends, requiring their approval in preference to a personal sense of achievement in a career . . .'[5]

Relationships are experienced differently by women and men. Women define themselves by their relationships; men are more likely to define themselves through their work.

Commentators such as American Nancy Chodorow believe this is because both boys and girls are brought up in their most formative years by their mother. Mothers, because they are the same gender as their daughters, find it difficult to separate themselves from daughters, but they do see their sons as separate. Fathers, because they have not been so physically involved with their children, treat both sons and daughters as separate. So, it is argued, femininity is defined through attachment and women are more interested in emotions and relationships, whereas masculinity is defined through separation and men are 'do-ers' rather than 'be-ers'.

Dana Crowley Jack argues in *Silencing the Self* that: 'Women's orientation to relationships is the central component of female identity and emotional activity.'[6] Unfortunately it does not seem to be the same for men; they are threatened by the very intimacy which women crave. Men tend to have problems with relationships, while women's fears are of separation and independence.

These theories, which are well supported by research, clearly illuminate a major problem in male/female relationships – poor communication. But they also explain why women suffer from low self-esteem and depression as a result of their concern with relationships. Until recently, theories of human development were based on *male* development. When women seemed to deviate from the norm, that is, from male behaviour, they were seen to be, at the very least, inadequate if not abnormal.

Women's dependency on relationships has traditionally been seen as unhealthy and a weakness; we needed to develop more self-reliance and autonomy, like men. Yet society depends on relationships in order to function: relationships between partners, parents and children, between different members of families, between colleagues, and so on. It depends on people, usually women, to oil the wheels of those relationships, and it is we who are usually the carers and the nurturers. However, that task is undervalued by men, and by society as a whole, so we are encouraged to regard our apparent 'dependence' on relationships as a weakness.

There is now plenty of research to show that strong attachments to other people are essential to women's well-being and continuing healthy development. However, those attachments have to be healthy ones, nurturing, empowering. Research also shows that supportive intimate relationships protect women against depression. Dana Crowley Jack observes that this is effective '. . . even in the face of stressful conditions such as poverty, inadequate housing, young children, or illness.'[7]

Unfortunately, too many women don't experience such healthy relationships and are therefore at risk of distress, depression, and low self-esteem. It is really not so very different from our essential needs for food and water. We may not die because we have lacked a close and nurturing relationship but, especially if this lack stems from childhood, we may be seriously harmed. There is plenty of evidence of the lifelong damage wrought by emotional abuse and abandonment, let alone by physical and sexual abuse.

Addicted to love

Some years ago, a book appeared called *Women Who Love Too Much*, which argued that many women are addicted to love and particularly to loving the wrong sort of man, the abuser, the alcoholic and such-like.[8] Written by American therapist Robin Norwood, it was hugely popular and created almost a cult following, with 'therapeutic' groups being formed for these 'love addicts'. Once again, women were being accused, this time by another woman, of being too needy for relationships, and therefore at fault.

Psychologist Bernice Andrews, writing in *The Guardian*

in 1989, expressed her concern that this book was simply reinforcing women's own feelings of inadequacy and guilt because they are with abusive men: 'The notion that such women are love addicts is potentially a very dangerous one since it can lead women to feel depressed and hopeless about their own supposed inadequacies. We are all equally entitled to love and to be loved and are not asking too much when we expect our needs to be met. Rather, we should be teaching the men involved in difficult relationships how to love enough . . . The need to be attached does not end in childhood but stays with us all throughout our lives, and is probably functional in promoting the survival of the species. There is evidence that the protection, love and support of those nearest to us is essential both for our mental and physical health, particularly in times of adversity. Love and support is especially significant for women.'[9]

Anna's story

Anna is the young woman we met in Chapter 2 whose mother always made it clear she was not wanted, that she was unloved. Not surprisingly, Anna has never had very satisfying relationships with men.

'I have had many relationships with men, and I always leave them. I'm always afraid of losing them, especially when I'm in love. That is completely traumatising, so it's easier for me to leave first.' Anna is currently with a man she does not love: 'This is much safer because there's really no risk of being hurt.'

Not only did Anna not have a good, nurturing relationship with her mother, but she never met any men as her mother hated them and wouldn't allow men in the house. She sent Anna to a girls' school and was very strict with her, refusing to let her have boyfriends when young: 'Fun and pleasure were dangerous things to my mother. Even when I left home, I'd feel terrible if I had a great weekend, I'd feel guilty and think I was going to lose my job.'

Anna is only twenty-seven. She hopes that continuing therapy will help her eventually to overcome her mother's dislike and disapproval and experience a good, healthy relationship with a man.

Christine's story

Anna always knew her mother hadn't wanted her; there were no family secrets in Anna's house, emotions were laid bare. Christine, however, sensed 'something was wrong' from an early age but didn't know what.

'I can remember at six years old walking down the road with Dad. I could always talk to him and I told him that I felt everyone else was play-acting and that I was the only real one. He looked at me with tears in his eyes, then said, "If you can tell me the name of that flower, I'll give you sixpence."'

Christine is now forty-four. She has been divorced for several years and has no children: 'There's been no other man in my life since my marriage ended because I have been so depressed and so critical of myself. I didn't feel good enough for another relationship after my marriage ended. Now I've discovered the great family secret, I feel angry because my parents cheated me of a family I would have loved.'

She now recognises that she has suffered from depression all her life: 'I remember as a child that people pitied me, they'd say I was plain unlike my pretty younger sister. My mother never said she loved me, though she looked after me properly. But my father told me he loved me all the time. Sadly this just highlighted the fact of my mother's silence. I was always trying to please my mother, so consequently I realise that I have this overdeveloped sense of always wanting to please people. When things go wrong, I always feel it is my fault and I'm always apologising.'

Christine was only nine when her mother miscarried a son. Christine quietly said: 'I was in the room when it happened. I was there for her.' Not long after, she was also in the room when her mother tried to kill herself by throwing herself out of the window: 'My father was holding on to her legs to stop her. I still dream about that.' When Christine's mother died, at the young age of forty-nine, Christine felt responsible, as she did when her husband left her six months later: 'I just felt it was all my fault. He was always out and he treated me badly, I now realise. He once told me I came about fifth on his list of priorities in life, yet we were married for fourteen years. But I tried to please him all the time, and ignored my own feelings.'

Ten years after her divorce, Christine's father died and her stepmother, quite deliberately, revealed the 'secret'; she sent Christine a bunch of papers, including her parents' marriage certificate. This showed that Christine, though born after her parents married, was conceived before. Her parents had not only lied to her but had given elaborate excuses for not producing their marriage certificate; they had even celebrated their wedding anniversary on the wrong date. She now began to understand why her family, especially on her mother's side, had treated her differently and why her mother had seemed to resent her at times. However, she did not make any link with this discovery when, about three years later, she again became seriously depressed.

'I assumed it was an accumulation of things, first my father's death, then I slipped a disc and lost my job because I couldn't pass a medical.' Christine then became 'very low': 'I was so tired, I just shut down, stayed in a semi-comatose state on the sofa. It was an enormous effort even to go to the corner shop.' Her doctor prescribed anti-depressants, which certainly helped, and referred her to a counsellor attached to the medical centre. After the first session, Christine was dubious: 'I wasn't impressed, she was very middle-class and didn't say much.'

She persevered and after three or four sessions, her counsellor explained to Christine what she saw: the impact on Christine throughout her life of the family secret, and then of the discovery of that secret.

'It was a complete revelation, and a release. Like someone

taking an axe to my problems. Everything fell into place. I understood why I wasn't given the same opportunities as my younger sister. I understood why my mother's family, which was terribly middle-class compared with my father's, didn't want to have much to do with us. I also realised how depressed my mother had been all those years, and it was completely untreated. My counsellor told me I would have to turn round and grieve again, for a different mother. 'I feel so different, in control for the first time. I now know my feelings weren't wrong all my life, I feel elated because I've at last confirmed the truth. There wasn't anything wrong with me. All my life I'd worn this mask, people didn't realise my true feelings, they thought I was super confident. Yet before counselling I was within a hair's breadth of falling apart.'

Christine's story is a very dramatic example of how early relationships influence us, and how our adult relationships are likely to fail because, as women, we do not value our own needs. We may not even recognise them.

Men who exploit our 'weaknesses'

All too frequently, women with low self-esteem seem to live with men who exploit their partners' lack of confidence, their lack of assertiveness. These men may also have low self-esteem but cover up their 'inadequacies' with bravado, aggression, laddish behaviour. They are not usually skilled in, or interested in, intimacy, but play on women's guilt and feelings of inadequacy.

Kate's story

Kate, now forty-nine, met her ex-husband when she was fifteen, and stayed with him until they parted some fifteen years later. He was always very possessive, and insisted she saw him every weekend when she moved out of their home town to go to college. He also insisted on their getting married as soon as she graduated. 'I thought, "Gosh, he must really love me if he's that jealous of me." I had no notion that that was wrong, that the main thing about loving someone is about nurturing them, promoting their wellbeing. Initially it was more a matter of survival.

'The first six years of our marriage were full of hope and delusion. I was living one little dream and he was living another. We never discussed our relationship. I just naively assumed we were working for each other's interests. For some years he didn't work because he wanted to write and I supported him. I didn't know I had any right to be angry about this, even when I discovered he was having affairs.'

Kate worked full-time and looked after their two sons. His parents helped them financially: 'When my first son was born, I didn't want to work immediately but nor did my husband. He'd been given an advance for a book. So I had to agree to return to work and he took my baby son to his mother's every day. She was very kind but I was terribly jealous, knowing that she would see more of my son's development, his first steps and so on, than I would.'

She supported her husband because she loved him and because she thought that was the right thing to do. Both her parents and her church upbringing had instilled this in her.

'I used to read the Bible every day as a teenager, and went to special service missions on the beach near where we live. I took rather negative thoughts on board: you mustn't be this, you mustn't be that. You certainly shouldn't try to impose your own personality and needs on your husband. It was all mixed up with the idea of vanity. You're not supposed to promote yourself if you're a woman, I was taught, not supposed to have ideas.

'I was absolutely sympathetic to his ambitions. You think they have talent and should have the opportunity to explore it. Then he would start another affair and I felt so unhappy. I still can't bear to read my diary from that time, it's too painful.'

Kate's self-esteem was even more undermined by her husband's attacks on her sexuality, claiming she was unsexy, a poor lover: 'Now I can look back with more confidence in that area. I know he chose to focus on our sex life, but the problem was much greater than that. He didn't show any concern for my sexual satisfaction. It was hard for me at times to feel interested in him sexually. I was very tired and he never showed any interest in me and my feelings. He had a very critical and abusive attitude towards me. He couldn't cope with my friendly nature. His prize comment was, "I might have affairs but at least I don't flirt." Nor did I, but I was open and friendly to people and he misinterpreted this for his own reasons. Now I know what I most wanted from him was affection. I didn't know this was normal, that I had some rights to expect this from a relationship.

'It's ridiculous to realise how I, and plenty of other women I knew, could get so hung up on small things and so quickly feel undermined. When my husband came home and asked, "What's for supper," I felt I couldn't say that I didn't know because I felt I had to be the perfect wife.'

Kate had tried to discuss separation with her husband for a couple of years, but he refused and she 'didn't have the energy to leave him'. Also she still loved him and kept hoping he would change. (If ever there were believers in miracles, it's women. We always think a man may change, even when we realise that the effort of *our* trying to change *for him* is damaging us.) But eventually Kate did leave, taking her two sons to live in the countryside.

'I went away from my marriage with very low self-esteem. And I felt that my sons, though only seven and nine, felt low about me too because of their father's influence on them. They laughed at my first boyfriend, for example. They didn't value me then because my husband didn't. I've been able to change all that and we're now very close.'

It is over ten years since Kate left her husband. She has been living in a small country town, with her sons, and teaching. She is a much more relaxed, more fulfilled woman, full of fun and curiosity, alive to anything life might bring. It has not yet brought a 'good enough' relationship, but she can cope with that and with her depression, which sometimes returns. Some therapy and co-counselling have helped, also years of self-exploration and talking with other women.

> 'One of the most helpful and illuminating people was a homeopath I saw some years ago. I told her how I got depressed and why, the awful marriage, fears of loneliness and so on. She understood me, she validated me, told me it was OK to feel like that. She explained that people want you to mend quickly. They don't understand that through my depression, I was exploring feelings, ideas, my past and my future. I still want to be with people but they have to realise they can't make me happy with a magic wand. Depression for me is about coming to terms with what is wrong in my life. I've learned to reflect: why? what must I change? Now I recognise depression when it comes, which isn't so often, as a process. It's not such a bad thing.'

Is it different for younger women?

Younger women today, in their teens and twenties, may be more aware of their 'rights' in relationships. Psychologically, they will have led less sheltered lives than their own mothers, and certainly than their grandmothers (who are still shocked by the frankness of the way relationships are discussed in the media). Therapist Toni White sees a difference in her younger patients' attitudes: 'Women in their twenties, early thirties too, expect more of life. They are less tolerant of depression. They have not yet created for themselves enormously rigid patterns of thought and feeling, they're more likely to change. So they're very motivated to have therapy.' She adds: 'They tend to come to me after a series of relationships with ghastly men. They often take off in their jobs whilst they are having therapy.'

> Margaret is twenty-one, a highly intelligent graduate. She knows she gets depressed when she doesn't have a boyfriend and she is also very aware that she doesn't necessarily conform to the female stereotype. But she is not yet confident enough to celebrate her originality; she sees it as another inadequacy: 'It's partly because I'm not very slim but also I find dealing with men difficult. I'm more confrontational and aggressive than women are supposed to be. I know most men find me scary. *I* find it all really scary. So I act like one of the boys, I'm not very feminine. I don't care too much about my appearance. People think I'm very confident, very much in control of my life. They're so wrong. I feel I have to go into the middle of the road and sob and scream before my depressed feelings are noticed by anyone.'

It isn't unusual for women to make such a comment. So many of us cope endlessly, putting everyone's needs before our own and pretending we're all right. I have wondered whether depression isn't an unconscious escape route for some women. Depression is in some ways total self-absorption and women aren't supposed to indulge in such behaviour.

> Joan is nineteen, in her second year at college: 'I do feel women aren't so scared as men about feeling depressed even though it's so painful. Men are not so open, and they don't want to hear about feelings. My boyfriend hasn't been sympathetic to my depression. He's not the most sensitive guy in the world. I'm learning not to share my feelings with him. He had no idea how to cope with my emotions after the abortion. He couldn't talk and he was obviously very frightened about me. He did say I looked like a shell with everything sucked out of me. That is how I felt. But most of the time now I don't tell him I'm low. I just act the fluffy female he feels safest with.'

'Fluffy female' is only one of the many roles women are

expected to play. No wonder we're often exhausted! Not only do women find juggling the various roles of wife, mother, femme fatale, and worker to be very stressful, but research conducted by Gallup in 1993[10] shows that their men fail to take this problem of stress seriously. They tend to say to their nearest and dearest, 'Pull yourself together.' A third of the women surveyed had consulted their family doctor about irritability, depression and insomnia; four out of five said they believed their problems of stress were far worse because their partners failed to show any sympathy or understanding. These are, no doubt, often the same men who make no attempt to share the burdens of home life.

Poor marriages: 'I'm drowning'

Many women feel they are 'drowning' in their marriages; they feel helpless and pessimistic. One woman of fifty told me: 'I try not to think about the future. I just don't know how to effect any change in my relationship, it all seems very bleak. I don't seem to be able to stop it falling into the same patterns as when we first married, twenty-seven years ago. I resent never having space for myself.'

Such feelings are common in the middle years of life, when children are growing up and we feel we can have more time for ourselves. We have to confront the prospect of staying in an unfulfilling relationship. For some of us, the 'bad boy', the affair, comes along. That may be enough and it may 'save' our marriage, because it makes us feel renewed, stronger, healthier. Then we can negotiate changes. But in many cases, the affair heralds the end of a marriage.

Gina's story

Gina is forty-five. She has been married for twenty years and has two teenage daughters. Apart from the first two or three years of marriage she has, she realises now, always been depressed: 'My depression stems partly from the fact that I feel unfocused. I have no great life plan, no sense of the future. I never have had.' She never had great ambitions for a career, though she worked before her children were born, and when they were older, as a teacher: 'Work does help. When I was at home with the children, I felt particularly depressed because I felt I had nothing to offer, no status. My husband didn't help my confidence either. He'd take me to parties and abandon me. They terrified me, no-one was interested in talking to a housewife. All the other women seemed so smart, so dynamic, managing children and a sparkling career. I often felt like an outsider looking in, not participating. I even remember feeling that as a child. I always felt that was depression. Life was a bit foggy.

'I also realise now that thought I had a very happy childhood, I was quite solitary because I was the youngest of five children. I remember feeling very cherished by my parents but I think they had run out of energy by the time I reached adolescence. My sisters would say I was spoilt rotten but I think I could have done with more parental support, a more secure framework in which to grow up.'

Gina knew for some years that her marriage was not good. Her husband had affairs and did little in the home. She decided she didn't want any more children but he refused to have a vasectomy.

'He told me he didn't want any more children with me, but he might want some more in the future. I didn't challenge him on this but agreed to be sterilised. I must have been depressed, but I certainly knew then the marriage wasn't any good. Why didn't I get angry? I don't know. The marriage certainly felt like a strait-jacket. My husband worked very long hours, and our life was geared completely to his needs. Like so many women, I'd sublimated myself to my husband and kids. I felt guilt at the idea of kicking against this. I felt powerless to stand back and assess the situation.'

Then Gina made some strong women friends: '. . . the great revelation of my thirties. I remember one of them sending me a postcard which said "A girl's best friend is a girl's best friend" and it made complete sense. I was at last given a chance to talk about how I was feeling, how scared and frustrated, about the children, about sex. I got support, I discovered I wasn't the only woman feeling this way. My women friends gave me the confidence I hadn't had before.

'I was looking for a way out and I had an affair. It was very passionate, very exciting while it lasted. He wasn't the ideal man but it gave me confidence too.' She left her husband soon after the affair ended and is now divorced: 'Now I don't get depressed very often. It's usually around feeling unfocused, perhaps if I have a weekend on my own and I haven't planned to meet friends. But I feel so much stronger. My depression was about feelings of powerlessness and helplessness. I never felt being a wife and mother were valued. I don't think my husband valued me either, though he'd deny it. I remember once going for a walk together when we were just engaged. I told him that I felt I was just his sidekick. That feeling never left me the whole time we were married.' Gina's story is not unusual; many of us put up with so much then leave in desperation. What she has learned is that living on one's own, or rather without a partner, is not the end of the world. She feels stronger and more valued, as she has built up a powerful network of friends and family.

Knowing when it's time to leave

Margaret was thirty-four when she got married, with a successful career and several affairs behind her. But being older, more mature, did not help her.

'I suffered from a low-grade depression for years when I was married. I just wasn't aware of that. I didn't know about other people's marriages and what I should expect. Perhaps I got married for the wrong reason, though I did love him at the time. But I wanted marriage as a sort of bedrock, a support. Then I could be even more successful with work, and have security. That's how I'd been brought up to see it.

'I admit that when my son was born, I was completely

absorbed with him. But my husband just couldn't talk about things, and sex was disastrous. He doesn't really believe in the importance of communicating. He'd say it ruined a relationship to be examining it all the time. He'd say that you don't constantly lift a young plant to check its root growth. So we didn't really talk, especially when I went back to work, encouraged by him, and we were both exhausted every evening.'

Margaret feels that the fact that they would eventually break up was 'unspoken' for years. It was as if they were waiting for their son to be old enough to cope. She questions why she stayed in the marriage for so long.

'Why didn't I get angry about the situation? Well, I couldn't see a brighter future outside marriage, I was too depressed, I suppose, and rather afraid. What would I be walking out *to* if I left? It was a bit of the devil you know being safer, and also an element of what was best for my son. And no-one suggested having an affair with me.

'You get to feel inadequate and unattractive living in a marriage like that. He was always saying, "Why don't you smarten yourself up?" I didn't feel powerful enough to get angry, or fired up about everything.' But two years ago, they agreed to separate and had a fairly amicable divorce: 'I realise I should have been brave enough to do it years ago. I'm not madly happy now, but I'm much more optimistic about life. I certainly have no regrets. I rarely get depressed and if I do, well I'd rather feel fed up on my own.'

Like Gina and many other women, Margaret has discovered there is life after marriage – or a long term relationship. In fact, she is much happier, despite a certain loss of status – and status doesn't keep you warm at night.

Fears of loneliness imprison us

It is of course the fear of being alone that keeps many women in unsatisfactory relationships. When people first separate, loneliness is a reality, exacerbated by worries about the children and about money. Separation and divorce often mean that women are worse off financially than before.

> Karen left her husband after years of an unhappy marriage, and lived with her children on a small income, tussling with him over custody and the divorce settlement: 'I don't think, though, that I was as depressed then as I had been before I left. The first three or four years after separation were a nightmare. I felt frightened, full of anxiety about money and how I'd manage to keep a roof above our heads. I don't think I stopped shaking for three years. It was a long time before I felt in control of my life.'

Yet one reason for separating was Karen's feeling of powerlessness inside the marriage. Despite the hardship of those first few years on her own, Karen is firm when asked whether she regrets the divorce.

> 'No, I don't for a minute regret no longer being married. I do regret some things about it. I regret the fact that I'll be poor in my old age, like lots of divorced women. I regret the harm it did to my children. And I'm sorry I haven't got my Joan Baez records – he kept them. But I don't regret much else.'
>
> Like many women living alone, Karen is anxious about the future, the prospect of a lonely old age: 'I guess I'd feel differently if I had a partner. Then I could look forward to retirement and sharing good times together. But I'm not sufficiently confident to do things like go on holiday on my own.'
>
> Obviously the prospect of a lonely, impoverished old age is enough to make anyone – male or female – depressed. But accept the reality and try to do something about it – find information about pensions, try to be clever about financial matters. And work on being brave enough enough to do things on your own. Maybe a fortnight's holiday is rather overwhelming. Start with a weekend on your own, somewhere there's lots to do, plenty to see.

The value of friendship

Leaving an unsatisfactory marriage or relationship takes its toll on our strength and resilience, especially as we feel we are now facing life all on our own. Female friends can be a lifeline, as Marjorie discovered. She was forty and had been married for nineteen years when she decided to separate:

'We had lived separate lives for years. He was a decent enough man and we had two lovely children. But work was his life, so there wasn't much left for me.' She realised, now the children had left home, that she needed her own life: 'If we'd stayed married, I wouldn't have felt able to have other relationships. I also thought I would never do anything for myself if I stayed. I felt it was now time to do some of the things I'd put on hold.'

Marjorie moved back from the suburbs to London and found a teaching job. She first moved into a house which she shared with other people, managing to keep her feelings of loneliness at bay.

'I made the classic mistake of having two casual affairs with two men. Both were younger than me, one recently separated, the other still living with his girlfriend. I just needed the attention. I'd turned forty and wanted to feel wanted and attractive. I was trying to prove something.' She then moved into a bedsitter and the more amenable of her two lovers moved away. She knew the other one was using her: 'I felt my flat was somewhere for him to go. He wasn't very interested in me as a person, didn't ask much about me.'

Marjorie's husband asked her to return, but even though her way of life was very unsatisfactory – she was lonely and unhappy – she knew she couldn't go back. She became very depressed, spending most evenings on her own as she knew very few single people.

'I took to having bottles of wine on my own. Most evenings, I'd go home after work, have about three quarters of a bottle of wine and then go to bed. I spent most of my spare time in

bed, I felt so depressed. I lost lots of weight as I didn't feel like
eating. When I felt really bad, I wanted to go into the middle
of the road and scream, "What about me?"'

The turning point came when Marjorie collapsed at work
and was rushed into hospital. The doctors discovered she
had a large ovarian cyst and performed a hysterectomy. After
such a major operation, weeks of convalescence is needed.
Marjorie couldn't easily cope on her own and might have
sunk into an even greater depression. But one of the parents
from the school where she worked arranged for someone
to visit Marjorie every day, and she and Marjorie became
close friends. She was also going through relationship
problems so they 'propped each other up'. They have
become firm friends, and are now both happily remarried
twelve years later.

'My friend took me out of myself. I'd never had friends like
that before, you don't so much when you're married. We went
out together, she helped me find extra work, and I made more
friends. She encouraged me to take up old interests such as
singing with a band. The lonely times were very bad but it
was worth going through them.'

Like so many women I've interviewed, Marjorie did not
regret her divorce. She had realised the value and importance
of female friendship, had managed to find her 'true self' and
had then gone on to have a more fulfilling relationship.

Trying to correct the balance

Women who find themselves still single around forty have
particular regrets to face. They may not have consciously
wanted a full-time relationship, but now they realise that

the biological clock is ticking away and that they may have missed out on the experience of being a mother.

> Jane decided she needed therapy when, at forty-six, she became severely depressed and was having very sad dreams which haunted and bothered her: 'I was dreaming about bleak autumnal landscapes, very empty. Just like my life, I realised, as I talked to my therapist.' She had a very successful career in banking, but her personal life was bleak. She kept saying to her therapist: 'I just don't know where the time has gone. I don't feel forty-six, but I've left it too late.'
>
> She had neglected her personal life, though she was, like so many single career women, godmother to many children. But she had very few close friends, another reason for choosing therapy. A long term gynaecological problem meant she had to contemplate a hysterectomy. She felt she had no-one to discuss this with, except her therapist.

Jane's therapist explained how sad it is for women like Jane to reach an age when they just don't have the same choices as earlier. Therapy can't help them have children but it can help them make sense of their lives and make changes in the way they live.

As Jane talked in her therapy sessions, it became clear that she had used her career as an escape route from a very stifling childhood. Her mother had suffered from depression most of her life and had spent time in hospital. Her mood fluctuated, and Jane never quite knew what to expect at the end of the day: a wonderful, loving mother or a woman crying in bed with the breakfast dishes still on the table. Work for Jane was a safe and reliable place. But she now realised that the balance of her life was wrong. It might be too late to have children but it wasn't too late to explore other aspects of herself she had neglected.

The feminist postcard of the woman crying, 'Oh dear I forgot to have children,' sums up the dilemma of so many women like Jane. The generation of women now in their forties and early fifties are to some extent pioneers. Born during or after the Second World War, we were usually much wanted babies and benefited from all the post-war changes. We lived through the famous, or infamous, sixties. We lived through the heady days of post-war feminism. To some extent, many of us thought we could have everything: single women could, for the first time, have sexual relationships openly; contraception was reliable, though it had its attendant health risks; divorce was easier so women didn't have to endure loveless or abusive marriages; there were more work opportunities.

But now this generation is contemplating growing older, in a much harsher economic climate, and we are assessing our chances of happiness and fulfilment. Some of us have gone through the worst, as in the cases above – they have come through separation, divorce and depression, and they set a powerful example. Not that romance doesn't flourish, too, for the fortysomethings. Many women, single or divorced, still hope to achieve a good relationship with a man, but are perhaps clearer in middle-age about the pitfalls and limitations.

Enjoying being single

Women who have come through depression and separation do often find they have regained their self-esteem and self-confidence. Louise, at forty-four without any permanent relationship, appreciates her new-found lifestyle.

> I would like to be with someone special but not at the risk of my emotional wellbeing and my self-esteem. More than once in my life, I have stayed with the wrong man, one who was

emotionally abusive, because I was scared of being on my own, without a man. I was in danger of losing all self-respect, let alone anyone else's, because of my behaviour and my fears. I also hate being celibate but what's the point of having a great time horizontally if you don't get on on the vertical?

'I now refuse to put up with appalling, selfish behaviour from a man. I like looking after the man I love but I like to be cared for too, and there's nothing wrong in saying that. I'm also trying to stop feeling it's my fault all the time. A mix of therapy and self-analysis have helped me feel this way, so much stronger, so much more my own woman. And I think that makes me more attractive to men anyway.'

Like many single women, Louise has a rich life – work, friends, family, hobbies such as gardening and the theatre. She will now agree with Erica Jong, who argues in *Fear of Fifty* that women writers should be able to extend their horizons beyond the love story, in the same way as women shouldn't only define themselves by their relationships with men: 'Most of our lives occur alone, or with other women, yet we are asked to shine a spotlight on the narrow part of our lives shared with men. It is not as if female life is all darkness except for that, but we are asked to pretend it is, and write of love, love, love – until it bores even us.' She sums it up rather neatly: 'That is what it really means to be the second sex. All your pleasures and pains are considered secondary to those you share with the other sex.'[11]

Ageing with optimism

Psychologist Bernice Andrews came up with some exciting findings on older women recently, after conducting research following a number of working-class mothers in north London. The research is part of a wider study looking at factors which predict depression.[12]

She found that as these women reached middle age, many of them were much happier with their lot, happier often than they had ever been. They had generally thrown off feelings of low self-esteem. Most had better relationships with their children and with their partners. Some had 'dumped' their unsatisfactory partners and remarried; others had made a conscious decision to have nothing more to do with men and were quite happy about it. Dr Andrews found from this study that good personal relationships were an important factor in these women's enhanced self-esteem, followed by success at work. Many of the women in her study had finally achieved this in middle age.

These findings are surprising, though many middle-aged and older women I've spoken to talk of feeling more confident, less concerned about other people's opinions, now they are more mature. But age does not automatically protect us against the misery of broken relationships.

Marcia, aged fifty, is still looking for the meaningful relationship – with another woman. She lived with her lover for twelve years and when they split up several months ago, she became profoundly depressed. She quickly met someone else and threw herself into that relationship, desperate for intimacy. That did not work either: 'I think I'm so desperate for the security of a relationship that I stifle my partner. I feel very insecure. I have this need to be the most important person to someone, probably partly because I've lost both parents. I also tend to gloss over difficulties because I'm in love with being in love, rather than the reality sometimes. Nor does it help being gay. I think heterosexual people really underestimate the difficulties of being gay in our society. How do you meet lovers? Who do you tell about being gay? Who can you trust?'

Her mood is exacerbated by her ambivalence about being gay, which obviously adds an extra pressure: 'I still think gay people aren't wholly accepted in society. I do think it's better not to be gay. I think something is lacking if you are gay, it's not quite normal. So I can't really blame straight people for thinking like that.'

As women reach their sixties and seventies, there are statistically fewer chances for them of meeting the perfect mate. Many will adjust to a single way of life with other pleasures, whether they have always been single, or widowed. It is particularly hard for the older woman who is abandoned by her partner.

After thirty-five years of marriage, Josephine was told one morning by her husband that he was leaving her: 'It came completely out of the blue. The shock was enormous. He hadn't met another woman, he just said that he wanted to climb mountains, to be on his own, without me. I was absolutely devastated and, for the first few months, suffered poor physical health as well as a major depression.'

Josephine is sixty-five and lives in a rather conservative part of Britain. Her pain was made worse by people's attitudes: 'I don't know many single people, everyone is married. Even my closest friends seem to see a woman like me as a threat. Or they're so embarassed about what's happened and can't talk to me. They're treating it like he's died. It is indeed like a bereavement for me.'

Three years later, she still cannot see her husband, but she has rebuilt her life and stopped feeling guilty, stopped saying, 'Why me?' She is beginning to wish he'd left years before. Then she could have started a new career, had more chances of another relationship.

Relationships *are* important to women's wellbeing. In *Social Origins of Depression*, George Brown and Tirril Harris found that one of the four factors which made women vulnerable to depression after some major life event such as death or redundancy was the lack of a close, intimate relationship with a lover.[13] However, it is also clear that unhealthy close relationships are a major cause of depression.

There are also many of us who are muddling along in relationships which, though not disastrous, are not very enriching either, and in which we have lost our sense of identity, of self-worth. If we are depressed in a relationship, we must look hard for the reasons. Is the relationship wrong for us, for whatever reason? Can we together make it work? Are we staying in a bad relationship because we feel terrified of being alone, that we have no existence outside the married home? If we can answer such questions honestly, even if that means separation, loss, more misery, coping with painful change, we may well, like so many women before us, become stronger, healthier, true to ourselves. Feeling bad for a while will eventually make us feel better.

Learning Points

If you're in a relationship and feeling low, consider these points carefully. Take your time and try to respond as truthfully as you can.

✔ Is it a healthy relationship? Or do you know in your heart of hearts that it would be better to separate?

✔ If you genuinely believe the relationship is sound, then examine with your partner the aspects which are making you unhappy. Perhaps he doesn't do enough in the home? Perhaps your sex life is not very satisfying because you're both always tired or you take each other for granted?

✔ What can you and your partner *together* do to change and improve your relationship?

✔ If you know it probably isn't right, why are you staying with him? Are you scared to be on your own and perhaps financially worse off? It isn't so bad to be a single woman. You can share with others or enjoy independence for the first time in your life. Better than living an empty, miserable life with the wrong man.

✔ Obviously if you have children, separating is more difficult but you must think hard about the pros and cons for them too.

✔ Does he exploit you and undermine your self-esteem? If he does, it isn't a healthy relationship and no wonder you're depressed. You have to learn to value yourself enough to get out. You're worth more.

✔ Are you kidding yourself, as women do, that you can change him? Forget it, most men – and women too, for that matter – cannot change fundamentally.

✔ The relationship may 'fail' but that doesn't mean *you* are a failure. It is sometimes very healthy to leave a relationship, and you will feel stronger and happier eventually.

✔ Are you depressed in your relationship because you're suppressing anger? Try to express your emotions. Ask yourself if anger is justified. If so, tell him.

✔ Are you depressed because over the years you've lost yourself, put aside your own needs and desires for your family's? Allowing time for yourself, finding your real self, is healthy, not selfish. It will benefit the whole family.

✔ It isn't wrong or pathetic to want a good, exclusive relationship – relationships are important for our mental and physical wellbeing. But be realistic about what such relationships can offer you. Years of romance, maybe, but often plenty of harsh reality. Knights on white chargers tend to fall off, and princes turn into frogs.

✔ Men have to learn to be better at relationships in order for relationships to be healthier and more rewarding.

✔ Value relationships with your female friends. They will always be there for you.

✔ Be true to yourself, don't pretend to be someone else to win a man, or keep a man. That way misery lies.

5 Body Image and Ageing

We have looked in earlier chapters at the particular pressures on women to conform to a female ideal – pressures which stem from early childhood conditioning and from society's expectations of women. I now want to explore what I believe to be one of the greatest stresses on women – the pressure to be attractive, to please other people, especially men.

In western society today, being attractive is mainly equated with good looks, with *physical* attraction; that is, a slim figure, a youthful appearance. Research by psychologists has shown that most of us equate good looks with a pleasant, good character. It may not be politically correct but we tend to assume overweight people are lazy and self-indulgent. Cleanliness is no longer next to godliness, but slimness is. Being thin also seems to equal success; we don't see many larger women among the powerful female executives and businesswomen.

There are growing pressures on men too, to look good, inevitably fuelled by commercial interests, but these are still minor compared with the pressures on women. Robbie Coltrane who plays the psychologist in the ITV series *Cracker*, can be seen as a sex symbol despite being overweight and has an on-screen affair with a pretty, much younger woman. Where are his female equivalents? Only to be found in comedy shows. If men have grey hair, it is considered to be distinguished; grey-haired women are advised to colour it.

We are conditioned from early childhood to be pleasing to others, and to value good looks and a slim body as the most important way of being attractive. For many of us, our feeling of self-esteem, of self-worth, goes up or down depending on how we feel about our physical self. This happens at all ages but is especially volatile in the teens and early twenties.

The tyranny of thinness

Most of us don't conform to the present-day ideal of female perfection, especially as exemplified by anorexic-looking models such as Kate Moss. Over fifty per cent of us take a 'large' size in clothes, that is, size 14 and over. None of us can avoid the ageing process, and many of us are terrified at the prospect of grey hair, wrinkles, losing our appeal, our sexuality. So, once again, women are confronted with a discrepancy between what we are and what we think we should be. This is a daily confrontation, given the ubiquitous media images of desirable women. We are again encouraged to be false to ourselves, to try to make ourselves fit someone else's expectations. And once again, we suffer low self-esteem because we are unhappy with our self-image; we confuse that with our self-worth. Almost every one of us has experienced the feeling that she is a 'better' person because she has lost weight. 'You're looking slimmer' is considered the greatest compliment, even though the woman being told this may look gaunt and unwell.

It is hardly surprising, then, that many of us experience low self-esteem, leading to depression, because of an unhappy obsession with our physical appearance. The most conventionally beautiful women can suffer from this; when they look into the mirror, they only see their 'faults', such as flabby thighs or a fat stomach.

This obsession leads to a wholly unnatural attitude to eating; food is the enemy, to be controlled and tamed. Our relationship with food can dominate our lives. Girls as young as eight are worrying about their weight and dieting. We can all count the calories in our sleep. If we achieve (I use that verb deliberately) the magic size 10, then our world will be transformed, as well as ourselves.

I vividly remember how excited I could feel as I started a new diet, whether it was grapefruit with everything or complicated configurations of food. I will get thin (although I was not fat, except in my own eyes) therefore my life will be rich. There was also some pleasure in being able, I thought, to control this aspect of my life, even if everything else in life seemed chaotic. The extreme forms of this obsession are eating disorders such as anorexia and bulimia, which can be fatal.

Susie Orbach is a psychotherapist and feminist writer, best known perhaps for her seminal book *Fat Is a Feminist Issue*.[1] She said in a recent article for *The Mail on Sunday* that a preoccupation with food is something women tend to take for granted: 'The first diet is almost like a female rite of passage. The young woman may be applauded for dieting by friends and family.'[2]

Quoted in the same article, psychiatrist Dr Richard Williams explains: 'Women's relationship with food can be seen as a continuum which goes in parallel with self-esteem. At one end of the continuum are the happy extroverts who might want to lose a few pounds in an ideal world, but are really not bothered by their size. [I don't think I've ever known anyone like that.] At the other are the seven per cent of the population diagnosed with full-blown eating disorders who have little or no sense of self. Then there are the vast numbers of women in between whose lives are dominated by some degree of thraldom to the thin body cult.'

Interestingly, a few pages away from this useful article on the 'thin body cult' is a full-page advertisement for an expensive cream to 'refine and shape the body's contours'.

What women say

Frances is thirty-nine, a talented and reasonably successful photographer. Since her mid-teens, she has been concerned with her weight and was constantly dieting.

'My preoccupation with slimming was linked to my lack of confidence. It was years before I felt I was OK as a person, as a photographer. Through dieting and buying far too many clothes, I was always trying to change my image, myself, because I felt the real one wasn't good enough. I can remember painful comments about my size. At school, one girl said, "You've got hips like plates." When I came home once from college, my father said I was on the plump side. I cried myself to sleep. He would have been horrified if he had known. It was a comment which made far more impact on me than anything he said about how proud he was of me or my achievements.

'For years, I frequently suffered from mild depression, often because a relationship wasn't working. And always linked with this was my anxiety about getting fat. If only I could be really slim, then I'd meet the right man and have the right sort of life.

'Now, in my late thirties, I look at old photographs of myself and realise that I wasn't at all overweight, but I wasn't skinny either, which we all wanted to be. I associated thinness with success in every aspect of life. As I went on yet another diet, I believed this time I would be forever slim, it was the key to happiness. My diaries reflect this concern, I dreamed about it. I have numerous diet books, and exercise videos. The essential problem of course was that I didn't have enough self-confidence in myself, and liked myself better when I lost weight. Not surprisingly, when I was really depressed, I stopped eating. Now I realise I partly felt bad because I was starving myself.'

Frances feels her 'salvation' was her discovery that regular exercise is much more successful at keeping her in shape than the endless yo-yo of dieting.

'Exercise also makes me feel better mentally and physically. There's a sound biochemical reason for that. However, I must admit that I still want to be slim and do weigh myself regularly. The other day, my partner said I was big, and I was horrified. He meant tall but all I could think was, "Be fair, I'm a size 12 now."'

Coline is twenty years old, a strikingly attractive young woman with long auburn hair. She has been depressed quite frequently since her early teens.

'It started with a feeling of being physically unattractive. I thought I was really fat, though I now look back and realise I wasn't. I couldn't talk about how I felt to anyone because I was afraid of being teased. I felt very alone.

'It is partly social pressures but also because I didn't like me, the way I was. The easiest way to change that was to change how I look, to lose weight, to have my hair cut, to buy new clothes. I'd throw away perfectly good clothes because I thought they made me look fat.'

Some women eat too much when they are depressed; it's an attempt to fill up that empty space, but it doesn't work. It becomes a vicious circle.

Jane is twenty-five and left university two years ago. She frequently feels low and lacking in self-confidence, partly because she hasn't yet found the right job and also because she doesn't have a boyfriend. She also feels depressed because she is quite large, yet when she feels depressed, she often raids the fridge: 'I hate myself for doing it. I know I lack confidence because I don't feel attractive, because I need to lose weight. I'm tall, too, so I don't feel very feminine and at times I act more like one of the boys.'

Jane does need to lose weight; she realises she eats a great deal and she doesn't have much exercise. She is usually slimmer. But she is often too depressed to go to the gym. Yet by regular exercising, she would release the energy she needs to overcome her depression and make changes in her life. In her case and many others, the pressures to conform in appearance, linked with other problems, have made her so miserable that she has rebelled and tried, however unconsciously, to make herself less attractive.

Dieting as a way of life

This female preoccupation with slimming is a peculiarly twentieth century phenomenon, partly because being plump is no longer a sign of wealth, rather the opposite. In the same way, most of us in the west consume more calories than we need, especially from processed food containing so much hidden fat, and we don't expend those calories in exercising.

The statistics on women and their desire to be thin are as distressing as those on depression. How much energy we would save if we didn't spend time counting the calories and despairing over our looks. Various surveys have found that far greater numbers of women say they are overweight than really are.

• American research shows that eighty-one per cent of

teenage girls want to be thinner, and seventy-two per cent have been on a diet.

- A London survey of schoolgirls aged around fifteen showed that about one third were on a diet.

- At least ninety per cent of women will have been on a diet at some time in their lives.

Louise, who is now forty-two, looks back through her diaries (written from her early twenties) and is equally horrified and amused to recall her obsession with weight.

'Alongside the concerns about finding the right man and the right job are the continual worries about my shape and my weight. Yet I was never seriously overweight and at times very slim. Every New Year, top of my resolutions was to lose weight. I've tried every diet ever devised. I've tried slimming food, slimming pills. I read endless articles about slimming. I had this idea that one day, I would become this perfectly formed, complete human being. Like, I realise now, someone caught in amber, or aspic. Only with age, and some therapy, have I realised that living isn't about becoming perfect full stop but it is about growing, adjusting, being, it is a process which never stops. Realising this, plus, I have to admit, living with a good man, has made me reasonably happy with my shape and my looks. It releases plenty of energy for other things too.'

The irony is that being obsessed with one's appearance can be very unattractive. Men don't necessarily want to be with skinny women and though they may seem to be obsessed with large breasts and never-ending legs, they are usually concerned with more than appearance. They find a woman's moans about her shape rather boring; they also notice the apparent imperfections they might otherwise have ignored.

Sadly, some women risk wrecking their relationships because of their obsession. These women suffer from a condition called dysmorphophobia, or the Imagined Ugliness Syndrome. The sufferers – women far outnumber men – are totally convinced that some part of their anatomy is hideously ugly. Many resort to unnecessary cosmetic surgery to correct the 'fault'. Others cover themselves up all the time, even from their partners. An article published in the *Daily Mail* in 1994 reported the case of a woman who felt her body was so repellant that she insisted on sleeping in another bedroom from her husband. She was reported as saying: 'I miss sex but I know it's my fault that it isn't good between us. Even when we were together my figure always got in the way – it just didn't feel right as soon as I got my clothes off. Seeing people's bodies on the television, people making love, upsets me because I just can't forget about my own body.'[3]

This is a rare condition, and obviously one where an obsession has tipped over into a major dysfunction. Similar, and sadly far less rare, are the eating disorders anorexia nervosa, bulimia nervosa and compulsive eating.

Eating disorders

Some experts believe anorexia has occurred in epidemic proportions in the past forty years. The Royal College of Psychiatrists has stated that one in every 100 secondary schoolgirls has full-blown anorexia. This is a disease which kills over ten per cent of its sufferers. Bulimia, the condition whose sufferers alternate between bingeing on huge quantities of food and then vomiting and/or using large amounts of laxatives, was unknown in the 1940s. The Royal College of Psychiatrists claims two in every 100 women aged between fifteen and forty-five have bulimia. But other experts dispute these figures, arguing they are too low and that as many as five in 100 teenage girls will suffer from an eating disorder.

The causes

Eating disorders such as anorexia or bulimia are called by some the 'slimmers' diseases', implying that women suffering from these have just taken slimming too far. Most experts would disagree. The truth, as we know it, is considerably more complicated. Unrealistic media images of thin women contribute to the problem; they can make girls feel very negative about their own bodies during adolescence, a time when their bodies are changing and developing. Many women who develop anorexia start with dieting, and may be slightly overweight. But they continue dieting to such a point that they often put their lives at risk. The Royal College of Psychiatrists explains that adolescents are very sensitive to society's and peer group norms: '. . . whether real or assumed. At a time of heightened sensitivity to the bodily changes resulting from or promised by puberty, it is predictable that young people will adopt society's concerns with physique and dieting. Furthermore, control of eating is one way of dealing with the inherent anxieties of growing up through creating an illusion of self-control.'

Feminist therapists Louise Eichenbaum and Susie Orbach have written that in anorexia, bulimia and compulsive eating: '. . . what we see are women trying to change the shape of their lives by trying to change the shape of their bodies.'[4]

Some of these women have been sexually or physically abused as children. Others may be trying to control or suppress their feelings about their parents' separation, or other problems at home. As the Eating Disorders Association explains in one of its useful pamphlets, anorexia is: '. . . an attempt to cope with living. It is a solution which is adopted for difficulties which seem impossible to resolve. Anorexia is an expression of conflicts about dependence, autonomy and control, and sufferers are particularly terrified of being out of control.' If we are frightened of losing control and failing in exams or relationships, by becoming anorexic or bulimic we seem to be 'succeeding' at something.

Rosalind Caplin wrote about suffering from anorexia in *OPENMIND*: 'Denying or restricting what she eats may be the first time in a woman's life that she takes control. Force-fed with values and expectations from family, school, society and peer groups, she may feel deeply inadequate to perform as an "ideal" woman. Feeling alienated from her body, she may be totally unable to express her grief, fear and hopelessness. She may not even be consciously aware of such feelings, but aware only of a desperate inner drive to take control of her destiny – to hunger strike in order to live and find her life.'[5]

The reality

'Emily' tells her story in an article on anorexia published recently in *Cosmopolitan*[6]. Unfortunately, it is an all too familiar tale.

I first started to diet when I was thirteen. At the time, I did not admit I had an eating disorder ... I was very intelligent then – the cleverest girl in the year. I used to get loads of stick for that. I also made friends with some girls who were getting involved with boys. So I was really torn between the academic stuff and growing up. I was really nervous in front of blokes and I thought that if I could lose weight, I'd be more attractive ...

'It's an insecurity thing. You get security from dieting. If I say I want to lose half a stone and then I lose it, at least I've achieved something. I also got security out of religion. I was brought up a Catholic. It's something people in religion have done over the centuries: causing yourself pain and offering it up to God. I used to tie ropes round my wrists and legs to stop the circulation.'

Frequently, young women who suffer from anorexia are high achievers, constantly striving for perfection and success. Outwardly they may seem confident and successful, but they are actually afraid that they can never be good enough.

Tanya was eighteen, in her last year at school and panicking about achieving good enough grades for the university course she wanted. She had become a complete workaholic. She had already started to diet, though she wasn't overweight, and that summer she started to exercise fanatically (the two often go hand in hand).

'I became an exercise addict partly because I had a lot of time on my hands after exams and also because I was obsessed with the way I looked. I think exercise and being able to shape my body noticeably gave me a sense of being in control of something, although in reality it was controlling me. I used to go to the leisure centre every other day, and do a full hour's workout at home the other days. This was seven hours a week plus walking fast whenever possible – nutty!'

In September that year, she moved away from home to college, and lost large amounts of weight: 'I think, looking back, that I had always been totally secure and cossetted at home so when I left I was very scared and felt completely alone, lost even inside myself.

'I didn't realise I had a problem at first, though now I realise I was a nightmare to live with the last two months at home and for my first three months at university. Anorexia meant that I lost my personality completely. I was completely exhausted mentally, mostly from adding up the calories of the food I was eating, which I would check and recheck twenty times a day. Physically, I was hyperactive and an insomniac. Often I found it a real effort just to undress at night.'

Tanya became a difficult person, quite unlike her real self: 'I became a liar, to cover up my calorie avoidance, and very violent when I became frustrated. I would even get annoyed with my clothes when I was dressing, punching my arm down my sleeve. I would be totally obsessed with little things, like people "borrowing" my milk, and paranoid about what my flatmates thought about me. Yet I was really sarcastic and short-tempered with them.'

Not surprisingly, Tanya didn't have many friends in this period and she recognises that men steered clear of her because she was so 'scary' and ill-looking. At the time, *she* thought she looked normal.

'If I think about that period of my life, I just remember feeling lost, cold and lonely, both physically and mentally. I don't remember any of that time in colour for some reason and I know I painted a lot of black. This is quite ironic when you remember that I was supposed to be studying Design, a third of which is about colour.'

Women with bulimia are often depressed; their binges may have started with comfort eating (similarly with the women who eat compulsively).

Judy was seventeen when she failed to get good enough grades for the college she wanted to go to, and when her boyfriend moved away to another town. She spent many evenings at home watching television, eating. Food seemed to be the only comfort she had, until she realised she had put on weight and soon she would be seeing her boyfriend. Disgusted with herself, she started to take laxatives immediately after eating, and sometimes making herself sick. She went into an even worse spiral of depression.

It was some years before Judy admitted she had a problem with eating and bingeing, and she sought therapeutic help.

Unlike women with anorexia, women suffering from bulimia don't necessarily lose huge amounts of weight. They appear to be eating normally and are very good at hiding their problem.

Whatever the cause of the problem, all these women who

have eating disorders (not to mention those women who come close to the boundary between obsessional dieting and disorder) suffer from low self-esteem and self-confidence. They feel out of control, or worthless. Therapist Jill Curtis has seen many women like this: 'With anorexia, it's as if the woman is saying, "I'm not good enough to take up any space."'

The treatment

Eating disorders are not easy to treat, even when the sufferer admits to a problem. The Eating Disorders Association argues for the importance of offering psychotherapy and other talking treatments, as the causes are clearly psychological. Research has shown that therapy, often allied with drug treatment, is effective for people with eating disorders. Unfortunately such help is not always available, and many women are admitted to hospital where the main treatment is forced feeding, drugs and a system of rewards and punishments.

Writing in *OPENMIND* Rosalind Caplin explains: 'An anorexic's statement is rarely understood . . . [These hospital treatments] serve to further disempower a woman, denying her her basic rights and may reduce her to the level of "a spoilt and naughty child". Unless she complies with the authoritarian approach and strictly measured regime, she is not considered "normal" enough to return to the community – in other words, there is still something wrong with her.'

Tanya, who became severely anorexic in her first term at university, did receive psychological help. She had two months of weekly sessions with a psychologist, spurred on by friends to seek help.

'This really snapped me out of it, first because he threatened to admit me to the local psychiatric ward, but after that, mostly because I had *admitted* I had a problem which I wanted to get rid of because it had ruined my life. I knew he had to help me do it as that was his job. So that was kind of like a secure feeling drawn from the knowledge that a professional was helping me.'

She feels her ability to talk openly about her anorexia to family and friends was vitally important in helping her too: 'I talked about it with anybody and everybody to start with. Once I'd confronted the problem and realised how stupid it was, everything fell into perspective and I started to have a normal life again.'

During the time she was anorexic, Tanya often became depressed: 'Looking back, I just regret the time I wasted being anorexic and depressed. Now I'm determined to live life to the full and I'm much more confident. I feel if I could get through that, I could get through anything. I still sometimes get depressed but it's no longer because of low self-esteem. Just sometimes I feel lonely and a bit afraid of not knowing what's in store. But I always manage to knock it on its head.'

'Emily' has not been as fortunate as Tanya. She has not yet received any help, and seems to believe she will never change:

'. . . when I throw up, I get a buzz. It's like being on drugs. The thought of being thin is a buzz. I know it's an obnoxious thing to say, but I know that my mind and body could not survive if I were overweight . . . You may not keep dieting for your whole life but the way your mind thinks can never change. I sometimes look at other people and wonder what it's like to have a life that isn't controlled by food.'

Eating disorders are obviously *not* a healthy response to society's pressures. But they are very much linked to the causes of depression in other women. Talking treatments, such as psychotherapy, can help women understand and resolve this. As one counsellor explained in a recent article in *Cosmopolitan*: 'It's so easy to become obsessive about food. Every family has to have their battleground and food is such a powerful thing. I try to persuade people that empowerment stretches beyond the body. They can control their lives in other ways.'[8]

Ageing

Our society's preoccupation with youth and physical perfection exacerbates our feelings about the process – the normal process – of growing older. It is particularly hard for women. Though a few women of forty and over are admired in the media for their looks, today the female ideal is forever young, with flawless skin and a slender figure, like a sexy doll. So, just as millions of pounds are made from the sale of slimming foods and dieting aids, older women are encouraged to buy creams and lotions which will, like a magic wand, make wrinkles disappear and imbue their complexions with a youthful radiance. I'm not being smug, I've fallen into the trap too.

But we shouldn't have to deny our age. We should celebrate the experience and, dare I say it, the wisdom we have accumulated along the way. However, there are obvious reasons for feeling depressed about ageing. In the west, older people – particularly women – are not valued: ageism flourishes at work, especially during a recession when it is cheaper to employ younger, less experienced people; it seems that men over forty are no longer interested in any woman over thirty-five; women who are separated or divorced in their forties or fifties will not be as optimistic about a new relationship as their younger friends; we face the menopause, and the prospect of other health problems, not just for ourselves but also for parents and others close to us; and many women face poverty in old age.

These are some of the realities of growing older; we must separate them from the myths. It is *not* all downhill after forty. Growing older is *not* all about loss, even though we are conditioned to believe this. Middle-aged and older women can be, and often are, attractive without having to spend huge sums on cosmetic surgery. With some attention to a healthy diet and exercise, we can be as active and fit as we've ever been. In fact, many women only discover the pleasures and benefits of exercise in middle age.

Mid-life crisis?

Forty, middle age (with all its awful connotations of spread and slippers), mid life – this is the time when, for most women, the fear of ageing really begins. This may be because we see the first signs of age – grey hairs, slacker skin – but also because it may coincide with our children growing more independent, with separation and divorce, redundancy and unemployment. These social and economic problems are very real, and may lead to depression. But as always, it is important to accept that these feelings are normal, a healthy response to unhappiness, or unfairness in society. But it is also important to recognise the dangers of becoming depressed about ageing.

> Marion is forty-nine, separated from her husband and nervous about the future: 'But I am determined not to worry about growing older, especially about looking older. My mother was very frightened of it and she always refused to celebrate her birthday. She'd say to me and my brother that she didn't want us to grow older either. I began to fall into the same trap just before I turned thirty. It's pointless. It's much better to accept our age even though I do find myself surprised at times to be so old.'

Both men and women complain of suffering from the mid-life crisis, when they may act rashly, or out of character, because of their fears of ageing. Men up and leave their wives for a younger model (and increasing numbers of women are doing the same). Men and women feel this may be the last opportunity to try things, such as a major career change or a dangerous hobby. They despair that the dreams of their younger days will never come true. In truth, it is rarely age which limits our choices but economic realities or relationship problems. The one significant reality for women is the menopause (see below) which does announce the end of fertility.

The analytical psychologist Carl Jung believed that a mid-life crisis is essential for people to take stock of their lives so far, and then to move on to a healthy second half of life. He argued that most of us lead 'unbalanced' lives for the first half, often necessarily unbalanced because of the pressures of careers and family, but at the expense of our spiritual growth. His biographer Anthony Stevens explains that at mid life, Jung believed: '. . . disagreeable though these disturbances are, they do have the psychological advantage of providing stimuli sharp enough to wake one up (for one has to wake up if one is to individuate).'[9] To 'individuate' is a Jungian term meaning to achieve the integration, or wholeness, of the personality.

If we accept there is a psychological imperative to change at mid life, however painful such changes may be, then we will gain a greater understanding of ourselves and lead a much more fulfilled life afterwards. We may accept our lot or we may embrace a completely new way of life. Most people wisely choose a path in between the two.

It is once again a matter of using our feelings of depression and distress to make those changes, internal and external, which will make us healthier mentally. So, instead of feeling miserable about the way employers discriminate against wrinklies, let's get out there and campaign for anti-ageism legislation, for example.

The menopause

The menopause is the major watershed for women at mid
life. All women will have mixed emotions about the end of
childbearing, but especially those women who have not had
children. The loud ticking of the biological clock is often
another cause for depression around the late thirties and
early forties. A real cause for depression, but not a reason
to rush into the wrong relationship or to become pregnant
without careful thought about what life is like for a single
mother.

When women are depressed at mid life, they and those
close to them automatically assume the reason is hormonal,
the Change, that time of life, that unspoken horror – the
menopause. Indeed, hormonal changes can cause feelings
of depression, particularly in the years before menstruation
stops completely (the perimenopause stage). But the picture is
often much more complicated than this. As I have explained,
the menopause tends to occur at a time when women are
already facing major challenges in their lives to do with
growing older, changes in family life, and insecurity at work.
The menopause may be only one piece of the jigsaw.

It doesn't help that the menopause is a subject rarely
addressed by anyone, except in quiet conversations between
women. (See the Book List at the back for a number of useful
publications.) We are afraid of it because we believe it means
we are no longer real women, attractive, sexual beings who
still have much to contribute.

Challenging our fears

In her book on the menopause *The Prime of Your Life*,
Pamela Armstrong cites the case of a doctor who had
an early menopause, aged forty, and who, despite all her
knowledge, felt very shocked. She explained: 'I was no

longer "fertile" and it didn't seem to be only a physical infertility. I felt it touched every part of my life. It wasn't only the ability to recreate with my body. It meant my creative intellectual life was also over. Somehow losing the one meant I'd lost the drive and potency in the other too.'[10]

As Pamela Armstrong comments, for this woman: ' Being "infertile" weakened her. Somehow she felt sidelined from the more "fruitful" world she had been part of up till then.' The feelings passed, and she is now leading a richly fulfilled life, but her emotions at the time were very real and are ones shared by many women. It goes with the territory, the notion deeply embedded in our collective unconscious that, after the menopause, women are useless, dried-up old crones. So no wonder we may feel depressed *about* it, even if not *because of it*.

Sue Pethen, a psychotherapist, has written (in an unpublished thesis on women and mid life): 'It is important to get biology into proportion with other issues – sociological and psychological – in order to assess the influences of each on what happens to women at mid life. Existential questions about life's purpose and meaning get confused with questions of roles and expectations.'

As Erica Jong writes: 'The astounding energy of postmenopausal women . . . is here, but the optimism to fuel it is not. The world seems ever more surely in the grip of materialism and surfaces. Image, image, image is all it sees. As an image, I'm definitely getting blurry.'[11]

There is growing evidence that the women now in their forties and early fifties – the so-called baby-boomer generation – are fighting back against the myths surrounding middle age and menopause. They are writing feisty, stimulating, useful books. They exemplify the truth that age does not wither us, nor put an end to useful, productive, enjoyable lives.

In a recent review in *The Independent* of *Secret Paths:*

Women in the New Midlife by Terri Apter, Polly Toynbee writes that the new generation of women is used to changing the rules as they go along, and they'll do the same about ageing. Many of them feel free for the first time: '. . . they feel powerful and influential. They have thrown off girlishness and ineffectuality, though sometimes only with a painful struggle when loss of looks and youth can feel like loss of power.' There is other evidence, such as Bernice Andrews' research quoted in Chapter 4, to show that as women grow older, they become less depressed.

As we age, we can also try to correct the balance of our lives, so that, for example, we don't allow our work to sideline our personal lives. It is a time to gain new pleasures, to enjoy new activities such as gardening or dancing, and to aim for a more rounded way of living. This must mean dismissing the power of images, of the material world. Erica Jong writes powerfully in *Fear of Fifty* about reaching fifty and the challenge it presents: 'We have come smack up against the spiritual hollowness in our lives. Without spirit, it is impossible to face ageing and death. And how can women easily find spirit in a society in which their most enduring identity is as consumers, where every struggle for autonomy and identity is countered by the relentless dicta of the marketplace – a marketplace that still sees us as consumers of everything from hormones to hats, from cosmetics to cosmetic surgery?'

Combating negative body image

We can work on ourselves at any age to deal with the depression associated with body image problems, and to recognise the pressures on us to look a certain way, to be a particular type of female. Do you remember what parents or other relatives said about your appearance as a teenager? Do you remember your reaction to what was said? Try to recall what you looked like; you probably weren't fat, but it's a fair guess you've always thought you were. Look at old photographs and you'll see that perhaps you were never overweight. Now is the time to rewrite your memories. If you are a bit bigger now, then plan some exercise and healthy eating, *not* a slimming diet.

✔ Look at the photos of models in magazines; most of these women are abnormally tall and abnormally thin. Some US research has shown that in recent years models' average weight has stayed consistent, but the pounds have been stretched over an extra three or four inches in height. And any 'faults' such as spots or wrinkles are airbrushed out of the photograph before printing. Clothes in photos do look better hung on a skinny frame, but that's not how we live a normal life. We don't stand around and pose but lead busy, active lives. And even on these thin models, the clothes are carefully pinned and tucked to look their most photogenic (just like the models!).

✔ I enjoy fashion and magazines as much as the next woman, but as I do, I try to remind myself that much of the copy is clever marketing. It is also unkind. Implicit is the view that we can achieve perfection; there is pressure on us to hate ourselves, our shape, our skin. Implicit is the view that we can improve ourselves by spending money – on slimming aids, slimming foods, new clothes, and cosmetics. Huge sums of money are made out of feeding our insecurity about our body image.

✔ For most women, our low feelings about the way we look may be only a part, though a significant one, of our depression. But we must realise that if we're unhappy with our body image, then our self-esteem will suffer, and that way lies depression. We must also realise that feeling low about our bodies isn't unhealthy, in the sense that it is a normal response to the pressures on women to conform to an ideal promoted by the media. What is unhealthy is to allow those feelings to dominate our lives, so that we're constantly dieting, constantly unhappy about our appearance. This is bad both for our mental health and our physical health.

6   Helping Yourself

You have to try. You see a shrink.
You learn a lot. You read. You think.
You struggle to improve your looks.
You meet some men. You write some books.
You eat good food. You give up junk.
You do not smoke. You don't get drunk.
You take up yoga, walk and swim.
And nothing works. The outlook's grim.
You don't know what to do. You cry.
You're running out of things to try.

You blow your nose. You see the shrink.
You walk. You give up food and drink.
You fall in love. You make a plan.
You struggle to improve your man.
And nothing works. The outlook's grim.
You go to yoga, cry, and swim.
You eat and drink. You give up looks.
You struggle to improve your books.
You cannot see the point. You sigh.
You do not smoke. You have to try.

Wendy Cope, *Some More Light Verse*

Wendy Cope's poem wittily addresses the dilemma all of us
have faced when we feel low and dissatisfied with ourselves
and our lot. But depression can also be so overwhelming that
it disables us, prevents us from doing anything, let alone some
activity which would help to bring us out of the trough.

I have tried to show in the previous chapters how various

experiences and events can make us depressed, although we may not understand or acknowledge the emotion. These events or experiences which affect us are mediated by our childhood conditioning, and by society's attitudes to women. Our depression is often a *healthy* response to an *unhealthy* situation, whether that be a poor relationship, problems at work such as fear of redundancy, or family difficulties.

But depression only remains a healthy response when we 'listen to' our depression in order to understand the 'message', that something is wrong in our world, at odds with our true self. Only then can feeling bad be good, because we use those feelings to gain understanding and to make changes, as the following case study shows.

> A busy executive in her thirties developed serious claustrophobia. She couldn't travel on the Underground in London, and then found herself unable to fly, yet travel was an important part of her job. When she saw a therapist for treatment of the phobia, it became clear that she was seriously depressed and that the phobia was a symptom, a reflection of her feelings of being trapped in a dismal marriage. Intellectually she knew she should leave but she felt guilty. Through therapy, she realised separation was the healthy option for her and her husband.

In this chapter, I will be giving you some practical advice on how to use your 'healthy' depression to make positive changes and become healthier mentally. I will also explain how talking treatments such as psychotherapy and counselling can help you.

So you're feeling bad

The first step is to acknowledge that your symptoms – insomnia, irritability, and so on – are signs of depression.

I hope that if you have read as far as this, you will have accepted your feelings and want to deal with them.

Don't feel ashamed of your depression. It is very common and very normal. It is telling you something is wrong, just as a physical pain might be telling you of a broken bone. What you have to do, and this will be painful, is to study every aspect of your life, in a thoroughly realistic way, to discover what is causing your depression. It is rather like undertaking an emotional audit.

Examining the present

Ask yourself what or who is making you depressed? Work with it, listen to it. Don't keep kidding yourself it's OK to sleep badly every night, or to feel tired all the time. You are worth more than that.

The reason may be obvious – a loss, through bereavement or divorce or unemployment – or it may be more blurred, a sense of dis-ease about the way you live your life. Perhaps you're in the wrong job, or working with difficult colleagues. Perhaps your relationship seems stale, or unfulfilling. You may be holding yourself back through fear of change or lack of confidence.

Or perhaps you have endured a recent change, what the experts call a major 'life event' which has forced you to rethink your life. Psychiatrist Colin Murray Parkes is an expert on bereavement, and has said in an interview that any life event which: '. . . requires a person to abandon one set of well-established major assumptions about his [*sic*] world and to develop another carries with it an increased risk to mental health.' Being made redundant, for example, is a hard blow to the ego and sometimes to one's wallet.

But its ripples and resonances, the effects on relationships in the family and with friends, the physical stress, are often undervalued.

Start off by asking yourself the following questions:

- Why do you feel as you do?

- What has happened in your life recently?

- What major changes have occurred?

- What have people said?

- Have you experienced any successes, or failures?

This task will be hard, but you must try to be scrupulously honest with yourself. If you have a close friend you can trust, you might suggest doing this together. They will have to be objective, which isn't always easy, and not blur your vision with their personal views and prejudices. In Chapter 1, I discussed the research work carried out by George Brown and Tirril Harris into women with depression in South London.[1] They noted four factors which made women especially vulnerable to depression after some loss or major 'life event'. These are:

- lack of a close, intimate relationship with a partner;

- lack of work outside the home (and so limited social contacts);

- three or more children under the age of fourteen, living at home;

- loss of mother before reaching the age of eleven.

Examining the past

As well as exploring your current situation, or predicament, look back to your adolescence, your childhood. If you're feeling low, you are probably also suffering from low or non-existent self-esteem. This, as I have explained, is a major cause of depression, and it is often rooted in early childhood. You can't change what happened to you in the past but by trying to understand how you were conditioned, how present feelings reflect past experiences and emotions, you should have a clearer view of your present predicament.

Sometimes the cause will be only too obvious; parental abuse, whether sexual, physical, or emotional, has devastating effects on children for their whole lives. But in most cases, parents have tried their best and shouldn't be blamed for what we have made of our lives. However, we can recognise that they instil in us their fears as well as their hopes, and we still hear their 'voices' when we are deciding what to do.

A forty-two-year-old woman Janet wanted to be more daring, to travel and even to work abroad. But she was scared and realised that, from an early age, her mother had imbued her with her own timidity. She had to learn to break free from this.

Alice Miller explains so well in *The Drama of Being a Child*[2] how searching your unconscious, the past, can help you (though we must remember she is specifically writing about children who have been abused): '. . . we cannot change anything in our past. We can, however, change ourselves. We can repair ourselves and gain our lost integrity by choosing to look more closely at the knowledge that is stored inside our bodies and bringing this knowledge closer to our awareness. This path, although certainly not easy, is the only route by which we can at last leave behind the cruel, invisible prison of our childhood. We become free by transforming ourselves from unaware victims of the past into responsible individuals in the present, who are aware of our past and are thus able to live with it.' Miller is writing about extreme cases, like Anna whose story you read in Chapter 2 and who suffered years of emotional abuse and neglect. But all of us who suffer from low self-esteem and depression can try to link it back to events and emotions from the past.

Women who are depressed often talk about feeling out of control, powerless in their lives. By making the decision to understand and deal with your depression, you are taking back control over your life. You are no longer a victim. You are confronting your feelings. Ask yourself: 'What have I to gain from being depressed? What can I learn?' Some people choose, unconsciously, to remain depressed because they cannot face the decisions they will have to make to become better.

> Angela knew her lover wasn't worthy of her, that he exploited her emotionally and was too damaged himself to commit to a fulfilling, healthy relationship. But she was frightened of telling him to leave because, she felt, her life would then be empty – no passion, no obsessive love or behaviour.

Recognise that you have lived some of your life by myths rather than reality (we all do this to some extent, and modern advertising and marketing feed these myths all the time). Judy Mann, in her wise book about gender differences *The Difference* writes that her generation (she is in her late forties): '. . . spent its thirties recovering from our adolescence and the mistakes we made in our twenties.' The mistakes were made – bad marriages, poor career choices and so on – because: '. . . we believed that a woman could not achieve genuine and lifelong happiness unless we had a man in our lives. What no-one told us is that there is no such thing as lifelong happiness and even if you fall in love with someone and have a successful marriage, you and he will invariably have to contend with periods of deep unhappiness occasioned by loss of loved ones, loss of jobs, illness. We were raised with myths, and the process of growing up became one of untangling the myths, sorting out reality from fantasy, and regaining our footing in the adult world of men and other recovering women.'[3]

Facing up to reality

We also have to confront certain realities: women are still seen as inferior; society sees maleness as the norm, not femaleness, not female virtues such as nurturing; both women and men face harsh economic realities. Many of us over thirty or thirty-five were raised to believe we would, given a decent education and hard work, find a job or career for life. We would progress, as our fathers if not our mothers had done. This is no longer the case and job insecurity can, and often does, trigger off depression if you are already feeling vulnerable.

When you have spent time examining yourself and your life, you will have a clearer picture of yourself, of your true self. Write lists, look at the pros and cons of situations, of a partner and so on. It can help to see it set down there in black and white, and it often helps to put your thoughts and feelings in some order. You may want to write down your dreams too, and learn to work out what they are telling you.

*   *   *

Your aim is to work towards being true to yourself rather than conforming to other people's expectations. Part of this should be an honest admission of your limitations, your frailties; we all have them. But don't be hard on yourself; women are usually nice to everyone except themselves. Equally, don't impose unnecessary limitations on yourself. Fight timidity. If you want to do something, such as a new form of work or a new hobby, work hard and systematically to achieve it. Accept the constraints of reality but not of your own making. As the novelist George Eliot wrote: 'It is never too late to be what you might have been.'

At times of anxiety or depression, I have found it useful to think through what the 'worst' could possibly be. For example, if I don't get a particular job and salary, will I have to sell my house? What changes will that entail? Once you face the worst, it takes away some of its power. I like the Gertrude Stein quotation: 'Considering how dangerous everything is, nothing is really very frightening.'

So you're feeling bad – that can be good

Once you have acknowledged your depression and started to explore the causes, present and past, you are, however slowly, on the way to being mentally healthy.

What is being mentally healthy? It cannot mean being happy all the time but it does signify having the ability and power to cope with life's ups and downs. Mentally healthy people feel reasonably fulfilled, or if they don't, they work to change that. They will gain a sense of achievement from small pleasures and battles, planting a few bulbs on a grey afternoon or writing a difficult letter.

Psychotherapist Jill Curtis, when asked about being mentally healthy, stresses the importance of finding an equilibrium inside yourself, and balancing your emotions. It is also about coping with and welcoming change; acknowledging life is a process, that we have to be flexible in mind and body, and spirit. If you look back to certain changes in your life, perhaps frightening ones such as ending a relationship, you may remember how exhilarated you felt afterwards.

> Jane had been miserable in her marriage for several years but in her late thirties, she felt powerless to change anything, and frightened to make the first move. One evening her husband arrived home from work and told her he was going to leave, because the marriage was so bad: 'I had to cover my face to hide the large grin. I was so relieved and now know I should have been braver, rather then wasting some years being so unhappy.'

Psychologists have been researching into what makes people happy, and although their findings are predictable in some ways they are surprising in others. Fame and fortune aren't the answer. Rather, as psychologist David G. Myers wrote in an article for *Psychology Today* in 1993 '. . . happiness is less a matter of getting what we want than wanting what we have.'[4] It is a matter of living in the present, rather than constantly day-dreaming about the future. It is about savouring the moment, the first cup of coffee, the first daffodil's appearance after a long winter, a call from an old friend. Pascal wrote of the danger of living in the future: 'So we never live, but we hope to live – and as we are always preparing to be happy, it is inevitable we should never be so.'

Think positive!

Research shows that people who are most satisfied with their lives, that is, happy, show four important traits:

- self-esteem
- optimism
- extroversion
- personal control

You can certainly learn to boost your self-esteem, to value yourself, and to take more control, even if that means some painful changes. It is more difficult to become more extrovert or more optimistic but as Myers explains, one of social psychology's arch principles is that: '. . . we are as likely to act ourselves into a way of thinking as to think ourselves into action.' So in experiments people who feign high self-esteem begin feeling better about themselves. Myers' advice is: 'Put on a happy face. Pretend optimism. Going through the motions can trigger the emotion.'[5]

This will not be so easy but, again, you could enlist a friend's help. The importance of self-esteem has been a consistent theme throughout this book, as it is throughout all the research into mental health. That magic ingredient so often seems way beyond our reach. Learn to like yourself more; list your good points! List your achievements, great and small. Separate your own feelings of self-esteem and self-worth from others, or from such status symbols as your partner's job or your children's exam results. You are a separate person, you have your own needs and talents.

Don't allow others to play on your lack of confidence. Recognise what and who affect your sense of self and self-esteem. Examine your feelings of powerlessness, and lack of control. As we saw in Chapter 1, self-esteem has been dubbed 'the immune system of consciousness', by psychotherapist Dr Nathaniel Branden, thus stressing its importance for good mental health.

Celebrate friendships

Spend time on good relationships; value your friends. Over the past twenty years or so, there has been a great stress on being independent, your own woman or man. We have been living in a very individualistic, materialistic and selfish society, where shopping, which can be a deeply narcissistic activity, has become most people's favourite hobby and therapy. You know the catch-phrase 'When the going gets tough, the tough go shopping.

There is growing evidence of the importance of close relationships for our mental wellbeing. Psychologist David G. Myers writes in *The Pursuit of Happiness* of a consensus emerging from: '. . . cross-cultural studies of individualism versus collectivism, from gender scholarship on independence versus connectedness . . . to preserve our social fabric we need to balance me-thinking with we-thinking. The social ties that bind also provide support in difficult times . . .' People who have several close, supportive friends live with greater health and happiness. In experiments, it has been shown that people relax as they confide painful experiences.

Like so much psychological research, this is stating the obvious, isn't it? Especially to women who have always recognised the importance of strong friendships, and have always worked hard to maintain relationships. As this work permeates society and government perhaps, at last, the female values (this doesn't mean men can't share these values too) will be rated more highly.

At the same time, recognise that some friends, work colleagues, acquaintances are not good for your health, especially at times of distress and despair. Some people seem to take a delight in other people's misery, without offering any real support. Some know how to touch on a raw nerve or are just totally unempathetic and smug. Don't feel guilty about avoiding what one stress expert called 'poisonous people'.

Tune in to your emotions

Learn to be kinder to yourself, and accept that you have needs and desires. What are you feeling guilty about? Is it rational guilt or imposed by some inner voice from the past? You don't have to put everyone else's needs first. Don't conform to expectations; revel in eccentricity if that's what you want. Take risks, don't always fall for the soft option.

Expressing your emotions is essential for good mental health. Crying can release some of the tension linked with depression. Older people may find this especially difficult, brought up on the ethos of the 'stiff upper lip'. One woman in her late sixties told me she had never cried in front of her husband because he: 'Likes things just so and wouldn't really know how to cope with my tears.'

Importantly, don't always suppress your anger. That way lies depression – or, at the very least, too many chocolate bars, too many cigarettes or one glass of wine too many. But if you're scared of your angry feelings, try showing them in private first; punch a cushion, write an angry letter and then tear it up or burn it. Go for a long walk and shout and scream your feelings to the trees. Eventually you will feel more able to be angry in a controlled and positive way. Then you can learn to say 'no' and mean it.

Be kind to your body

Recognise the strong links between your mind and your body. There is clear evidence that mental stress and depression can affect your physical health, and similarly, that the way we treat our bodies influences our mental health. So, recognise unhealthy attitudes to diet, body image, ageing. You can make more effective, and healthier, changes to your life than starving yourself or having a facelift.

Eat well

Eat healthily – plenty of fruit, vegetables, low-fat foods. Don't follow cranky or calorie counting diets. If you're seriously overweight, ask for medical help and only follow a diet if it is sensible, not a matter of starvation, and make sure you exercise at the same time.

Learn about the specific effects of certain foods. For example, certain foods may help beat depression. Depressed people are known to suffer from low levels of serotonin, a substance in the brain thought to be implicated in depression as a mood raiser and natural tranquilliser. So eat plenty of foods rich in tryptophan, an amino acid which the brain converts into serotonin. These foods include turkey, peanuts, lamb's liver, milk and mangoes. Foods which contain stress-reducing substances are also vital; these include fresh fruit and vegetables.

Avoid alcohol and cigarettes

Do not drink too much alcohol. A few drinks may temporarily lift your mood but alcohol is bad for your physical and mental health *and* it is a depressant. It also gives you hangovers, provides useless calories and stops you sleeping. Cigarettes are also used to 'fill the hole' when we are depressed. But they're not much good for our mental health, and very bad for our physical health.

Learn to enjoy exercise

Exercise is a brilliant antidote to feeling low. Vigorous exercise stimulates the body into releasing endorphins, the body's natural anti-depressants. Exercise also counters stress, which can often lead to, or add to, depression. Try to exercise at least three times a week, even if it's just a brisk thirty-minute walk. There is consistent research evidence that moderate exercise increases mental as well as physical wellbeing. Exercise increases your metabolic rate, so you burn up more calories – whereas years of chronic dieting actually lower your metabolic rate. Choose some form of exercise which you enjoy, then you will keep it up. Walking is a good exercise which is free and can easily be fitted into a busy life. You don't have to, and shouldn't, become addicted to the gym or jogging for miles. This just adds extra stress.

You can use exercise as a potent 'drug' which regulates weight, strengthens bones and reduces the risk of osteoporosis, makes the heart stronger and so protects against heart attacks, and makes you more flexible and mobile. It immediately makes you feel emotionally better and, over time, can give you a stronger sense of self-confidence and self esteem, perhaps especially for women over forty.

However, I do accept that when you feel very depressed, it is a huge effort to go for a short walk let alone go to a gym or an aerobics class. Set yourself some form of exercise as a weekly task and, even better, enlist the company of a friend. There is nothing like a bit of friendly competition and encouragement to start exercising regularly.

Learn to relax

Learn to recognise the effects of stress, which often complicates and exacerbates depression. Learn relaxation techniques, such as meditation, or deep breathing exercises. These can help you sleep better too. Treat yourself to activities which relax and please you; a soak in a warm, sweet-smelling bath, listening to favourite music, a visit to an art gallery, reading an involving novel. Learn to use aromatherapy – differently scented oils to relax or stimulate you. Encourage your partner, if you have one, to give you a relaxing message.

Insomnia is a classic symptom of depression and stress. Research again shows that enough sleep and general rest are vital to mental health. Rather than relying on sedatives, which can make you feel drowsy *and* depressed the next day, learn deep breathing exercises and work out a routine which is more conducive to sleep. Don't eat too soon before going to bed. Try warm milky drinks (milk is a good food for helping you unwind). If you really can't sleep, try not to panic but make yourself some herbal tea and read a light novel. If your mind is racing stressfully about all you have to do, or about specific problems, make lists. This helps you order your troubled thoughts and may help you go back to sleep once they are committed to paper.

Talking treatments

However hard you try to help yourself, you may feel the need for outside help, and there is no shame in this. So many women and men have been helped through their depressions and other mental conditions with the help of psychotherapy and counselling.

Put simply, the 'talking treatments' such as psychotherapy

will help you resolve the internal, sometimes unconscious conflicts which are causing your depression. They can help you make the links between past and present, as discussed earlier, and identify the unconscious barriers and emotions which are crippling you. I have interviewed many people who have found these treatments very successful in dealing with their depression.

As one woman said to me, it is much easier to talk to a stranger – a therapist or counsellor – when you are feeling vulnerable. There is strictly no emotional involvement and you don't have to put on a good image. Rather the reverse; the therapist wants to see the real you. Therapist Mary Edwards told me she saw part of her job as being 'a container' for the terrible pain and anguish which patients may bring up during a session. Therapists can also offer an objective view which even the best of friends may find difficult.

Therapy should help you understand the emotions which are controlling you – anger, loss and so on – and work towards you taking control of yourself. Then you will be able to build up your self-esteem and self-confidence, and plan the life you want.

Aim to be your true self. It can liberate you from unhealthy feelings and patterns of behaviour. It won't bring eternal happiness, it won't bring you back your partner or your job, but it will strengthen you to deal better with these losses.

Depending on the type of therapy, treatment may be anything from a few sessions of counselling to several years of psychoanalysis, the in-depth therapy where a patient usually sees the analyst four or five times a week.

Unlike drugs, therapy aims to help you make sense of, to understand, the reasons for your depression and misery. It is a humane form of treatment, respecting people as individuals.

Finding the right therapist

I have listed some of the main therapy organisations in the Resource Guide at the back of the book. Unfortunately it is not easy to find therapy on the NHS, though a growing number of medical centres have counsellors attached. Otherwise, you will probably have to pay, and fees vary widely. It is advisable to find a therapist or counsellor through a known organisation whose members will be accountable and adhere to certain training requirements. Remember that it is still not mandatory for someone claiming to be a counsellor or therapist to undergo formal training or to belong to any professional body with a code of ethics and a code of practice.

Drugs

Too many women are simply prescribed drugs when they visit their family doctor. These are usually anti-depressants and, though they do work, many have unpleasant side-effects and do not reach the root of the problem. Some doctors still prescribe minor tranquillisers, such as Valium, for depression. But not only are these addictive, they can also increase depression.

The group of anti-depressants known as tricyclics (brand names include Tofranil and Anafranil) appear to act on the biochemical pathways inside the brain to restore a person's mood to normal. They often take up to two weeks to have any effect and they have side-effects such as drowsiness and nausea. Therapist Toni White advises only taking anti-depressants as a last form of defence: 'Feelings become less intense so it's hard to do therapy, it's like working through a fog.'

There is a newer group of anti-depressants, the serotonin specific re-uptake inhibitors (SSRIs). These, as their name implies, work to prevent the lowering of the serotonin levels in the brain; serotonin is a sort of natural anti-depressant. The best known of this group is the apparently miraculous drug Prozac which is prescribed for all sorts of conditions, including 'compulsive' shopping, as well as depression. I have interviewed several women who have found that Prozac lifted their depression and made them feel very well. However, these are new drugs and some experts would warn about unknown side-effects.

There are therapists who are prepared to work with patients taking Prozac and similar drugs, because they don't sedate people, or make them unresponsive to therapy. If your depression is so crippling, the combination of a drug such as Prozac (or another of the SSRIs) and psychotherapy could be the answer. As therapy begins to work, then the drug can be discontinued.

Stepping out

It is so much easier to give advice than to take it. I have tried most of the options described above, including psycho-therapy which I have found very useful, as a short-term and a longer-term treatment. Done well, therapy gives you a way of looking at, and hopefully resolving, life's problems unlike any other. It gives you an extra dimension on the world. It isn't a miracle cure, but it should make you stronger and braver.

In this chapter I've tried to show you some simple steps towards counteracting depression, such as building some exercise into your daily routine. You'll find suggestion for further reading in the Book List at the back of this book if you'd like to explore some of the actions I've described. Work out ways of beating depression when you're in a good mood; write a list, and try hard to put it into practice when you're depressed. One woman I know takes herself off to the country because she knows how urban life, with the noise, the stress, the pollution, exacerbates her low mood; another will seek solace in her garden. Work out which strategies work best for you – and put them into practice.

Most importantly, don't be afraid of change or of making mistakes. I'll leave you with a favourite quotation from an elderly American, Nadine Stair.[6] I think she is very wise.

If I had my life to live over, I'd dare to make more mistakes next time. I'd relax. I'd limber up. I would be sillier than I have been this trip. I would take fewer things seriously. I would take more chances. I would take more trips. I would climb more mountains and swim more rivers. I would eat more ice cream and less beans. I would perhaps have more actual troubles, but I'd have fewer imaginary ones.

You see, I'm one of those people who live sensibly and sanely hour after hour, day after day. Oh, I've had my moments and, if I had it to do over again, I'd have more of them. In fact, I'd try to have nothing else. Just moments, one after another, instead of living so many years ahead of each day. I've been one of those persons who never goes anywhere without a thermometer, a hot water bottle, a raincoat and a parachute. If I had to do it again, I would travel lighter than I have.

If I had my life to live over, I would start barefoot earlier in the spring and stay that way later in the fall. I would go to more dances. I would ride more merry-go-rounds. I would pick more daisies.

Nadine Stair, Louisville, Kentucky

References

Introduction

1. Chapter on 'Women and mental illness,' by Dr Rachel Jenkins, in *Promoting Women's Health*, the report of a conference, King's Fund, 1990.
2. *Eve fights back*, by Katherine Darton, Janet Gorman and Liz Sayce. MIND Publications, 1994.
3. *Social Focus on Women*. Central Statistical Office, HMSO, 1995.
4. *Expectations for the future: an investigation into the self-esteem of 13 and 14 year old girls and boys*, Health Education Authority, 1995.

Chapter 1: What Depression Feels Like

1. E.S. Paykel, R. G. Priest. British Medical Journal. 305. 14, November 1992.
2. *Mental Illness: The fundamental facts*. The Mental Health Foundation, 1993.
3. Sigmund Freud. *Five Lectures on Psychoanalysis* in *Two Short Accounts of Psychoanalysis*, Penguin.
4. Heather Ashton. *Psychotropic-Drug Prescribing for Women*, British Journal of Psychiatry (158), 1991.
5. *Social Focus on Women*, CS, HMSO, 1995.
6. Dorothy Rowe. 'Why it's the good girls who get depressed'. *The Mail on Sunday*, 16 November 1994.
7. Alice Miller. *The Drama of Being a Child*, Virago. 1995.
8. M. Scott Peck. *The Road Less Travelled*, Arrow, 1990.
9. Richard B. Fisher. *A Dictionary of Mental Health*, Granada, 1980.

10. Research by Bem (1974.5), quoted in *Working With Depressed Women*, Gower Press, 1987.
11. Nathaniel Branden. *Six Pillars of Self-Esteem*, Bantam, 1995.
12. George W. Brown and Tirril Harris. *Social Origins of Depression*, Tavistock, 1979.
13. The Minnesota Study of Twins Reared Apart, begun in 1979 by psychologist Dr Thomas J. Bouchard, quoted in *The Difference*, Judy Mann, Warner, 1994.
14. Alice Miller. *The Drama of Being a Child*, Virago, 1995.

Chapter 2: Why Can't A Woman Be More Like A Man?

1. Judy Mann. *The Difference, Growing Up Female in America*, Warner, 1994.
2. *Expectations for the Future. An investigation into the self-esteem of 13 and 14 year old girls and boys*, Health Education Authority, 1995.
3. *Evening Standard*, 19 July 1995.
4. Research quoted in Mann, ibid.
5. Dr Nathanial Branden. *Six Pillars of Self-Esteem*, Bantam, 1994.
6. Mann, ibid.
7. Branden, ibid.
8. Branden, ibid.
9. Pamela Ashurst and Zaida Hall. *Understanding Women in Distress*, Tavistock/Routledge, 1989.
10. Louise Eichenbaum and Susie Orbach. *Understanding Women*, Penguin, 1985.
11. Ashurst and Hall, ibid.
12. B. Andrews, G.W. Brown and L. Creasey. *Intergenerational Links between Psychiatric Disorders in Mothers and Daughters: The Role of Parenting Experiences*, J. Child Psychol. Pyschiat. Vol. 31. No. 7, 1990.
13. Hope Edelman. *Motherless Daughters*, Hodder and Stoughton, 1994.

Chapter 3: Women in Society Today – Still The Outsiders?

1. Kate Figes. *Because of her sex*, Pan, 1994.
2. *Social Focus on Women*. Central Statistical Office. HMSO. 1995.

3. *The Guardian*, 9 August 1995.
4. Ibid.
5. Research quoted in *The Guardian*, October 22 1994.
6. *The Telegraph Magazine*, 19 August 1995.
7. Jill Rubery. *The Gender Pay Gap: Some European Comparisons*, 1993.
8. *Social Focus on Women*, ibid.
9. *Health Survey for England*, 1993. HMSO.
10. ILO Report quoted in *The Guardian*, August 25 1995.
11. *New Internationalist*, August 1995.

Chapter 4: The Importance of Relationships.

1. Erica Jong. *Fear of Fifty*, Chatto and Windus, 1994.
2. Caroline Heilbrun. *Writing a Woman's Life*, Ballantine, 1988.
3. Dana Crowley Jack. *Silencing the Self. Women and Depression*, Harvard University Press, 1991.
4. *The Guardian*, 19 August 1995.
5. Pamela Ashurst and Zaida Hall. *Understanding Women in Distress*, Tavistock/Routledge, 1989.
6. Dana Crowley Jack. *Silencing the Self. Women and Depression*, Harvard University Press, 1991.
7. Ibid.
8. Robin Norwood. *Women Who Love Too Much*, Arrow, 1985.
9. *The Guardian*, 23 May 1989.
10. *Gallup Survey*, 1993.
11. Erica Jong. *Fear of Fifty*, Chatto and Windus, 1994.
12. *Stability and change in low self-esteem: the role of psychosocial factors*. Bernice Andrews and George W. Brown. Psychological Medicine, 25. 1995.
13. George W. Brown and Tirril Harris. *Social origins of Depression*, Tavistock, 1978.

Chapter 5: Body Image and Ageing

1. Susie Orbach. *Fat is a feminist Issue*, 1982.
2. *The Mail on Sunday*, 16 July 1995.
3. *The Daily Mail*, 18 January 1994.
4. Louise Eichenbaum and Susie Orbach. *Understanding Women*, Penguin, 1983.
5. OPENMIND, Dec 1991/January 1992.
6. *Cosmopolitan*, September 1995.

7. OPENMIND, Dec 1991/Jan 1992.
8. *Cosmopolitan*, Sept 1995.
9. Anthony Stevens. *On Jung*, Routledge, 1990.
10. Pamela Armstrong. *The Prime Of Your Life*, Headline, 1995.
11. Erica Jong. *Fear of Fifty*, Chatto and Windus, 1994.
12. *The Independent*, October 1995. (Review of *Secret Paths: Women in the New Midlife*, Terri Apter, Norton 1995).
13. Erica Jong. *Fear of Fifty*, Chatto and Windus, 1994.

Chapter 6. Helping Yourself.

1. George W. Brown and Tirril Harris. *Social origins of Depression*, Tavistock, 1978.
2. Alice Miller. *The Drama of Being a Child*, Virago, 1995.
3. Judy Mann. *The Difference*, Warner, 1994.
4. *Psychology Today*, July/August 1993.
5. Ibid.
6. E.A. Charlesworth and R.G. Nathan. *Stress Management – A Comprehensive guide to Wellness*, Souvenir Press, 1986.

Further Reading

Depression

Depression. The way out of your prison, Dorothy Rowe, RKP.
The experience of depression, Dorothy Rowe, John Wiley.

Personal accounts

Other women, Lisa Alther, Penguin.
The words to say it, Marie Cardinal, Women's Press.
A guard within, Sarah Ferguson, Flamingo.
August, Judith Rossner, Coronet.

Women's psychology

Women and madness, Phyllis Chesler, Avon.
Women who run with the wolves. Myths and stories of the wild woman archetype, Clarissa Pinkola Estes.
In a different voice, Carol Gilligan, Harvard University Press.
Moving beyond words, Gloria Steinem, Simon and Schuster.
Revolution from within, A book of self-esteem, Gloria Steinem.

General psychology/relationships

Men are from Mars, women are from Venus, John Gray, Thorsons.
The end of marriage, Dr Julian Hafner, Century.

Jocasta's children. The imprint of the mother, Christiane Olivier, Routledge.
You just don't understand. Women and men in conversation, Deborah Tannen, Ballantine.

Eating disorders/body image

Fed up and hungry. Women, oppression and food, Ed. Marilyn Lawrence, Women's Press.
Feasting and fasting, Paulette Maisner and Jenny Pulling, Fontana.
Hunger Strike, Susie Orbach, Penguin.
The beauty myth, Naomi Wolf, Vintage.

Mid-life issues and menopause

Ourselves, growing older: Women aging with knowledge and power, Paula Brown Doress and Diana Laskin Siegal, Simon Schuster.
The change, Germaine Greer, Penguin.
The silent passage, Gail Sheehy.
In midlife. A Jungian perspective, Murray Stein, Spring Publications.

Psychotherapy

Talking to a stranger, Lindsay Knight, Hodder and Stoughton.
A complete guide to therapy, Joel Kovel, Penguin.

Self-help

Intimacy and solitude, Stephanie Dowrick, Women's Press.
Listening to Prozac, Peter D. Kramer, Fourth Estate.
The complete guide to psychiatric drugs, Ron Lacey, Ebury Press/MIND.
Making sense of treatments and drugs: Anti-depressants, MIND.

Resource Guide

Relationships

Single Concern Group
PO Box 4
High Street
Goring-on-Thames
Oxon RG8 9DN

01491 873195

Helps lonely and socially isolated people; publishes magazines to enable people to make contact with each other and with professional and voluntary workers who run a telephone link and help service. Volunteers specialise in agoraphobia, bulimia/anorexia, depression, bereavement, divorce, single parenthood, loneliness and related problems.

National Stepfamily Association
Chapel House
18 Hatton Place
London ECIN 8JH

0171 209 2460
0171 209 2464 (counselling line)

Offers telephone counselling, advice and support for all members of stepfamilies; encourages the development of self-help groups nationwide; maintains data on therapists willing to help stepfamilies.

Parent Network
44–46 Caversham Road
London NW5 2DS

0171 485 8535

Provides support and education groups for parents (called Parent-Link) in their local areas, which offer suggestions for handling challenges and difficulties in family life; aims to help parents and children feel better about themselves and each other. Also trains and supports parents to run Parent-Link groups.

Bereavement

Cruse (bereavement care)
Cruse House
126 Sheen Road
Richmond
Surrey TW9 1UR

0181 940 4818
0181 332 7227 (bereavement line)

Offers free help to bereaved people through a network of 192 branches; individual and group counselling; practical advice and social contact.

The Compassionate Friends
53 North Street
Bristol BS3 1EN

0117 966 5202
0117 953 9639 (helpline)

Friendship and support offered to newly bereaved families by bereaved parents. Help given to grieving parents who have lost a child of any age including adult through illness, murder, suicide or accident.

Cot Death Society
1 Browning Close
Thatcham
Berks RG18 3EF

01635 861771

24-hour information service for parents; provides respiration monitors to help preserve the lives of those at risk together with training, back-up and counselling.

Stillbirth and Neonatal Death Society
28 Portland Place
London W1N 4DE

0171 436 7940
0171 436 5881 (helpline)

Offers support and friendship to parents bereaved through late pregnancy loss, stillbirth and neonatal death. Runs over 200 self-help groups nationwide; provides information and a range of published material including a newsletter.

Self-help

Samaritans
10 The Grove
Slough
Berks SL1 1QP

01753 532713

The Samaritans offer a 24-hour confidential telephone support service for people who are depressed and suicidal through 199 centres in the UK and Eire. The volunteers at each centre work under the guidance of a volunteer director who takes the advice of a consultant psychiatrist when necessary.

Families

PARENTLINE
Endway House,
The Endway
Hadleigh
Essex SS7 2AN

01702 554782
01702 559900 (helpline)

Provides support for parents experiencing stress; maximises the family's capacity to care for its child; helplines and drop-in centres; a network of 26 groups for stressed parents; professional back-up available.

Family Crisis Line
c/o Ashwood House
Ashwood Road
Woking
Surrey GU22 7JW
01483 722533

Provides a confidential telephone support service for people experiencing any form of domestic crisis or stressful situation. The line is staffed by trained volunteers.

Association for Post-Natal Illness
25 Jerdan Place
London SW6 1BE

0171 386 0868

Supports and advises women suffering from post-natal depression; runs a network of volunteers who offer help to sufferers nationwide.

Exploring Parenthood
4 Ivory Place
20a Treadgold Street
London W11 4BP

0171 221 4471
0171 221 6681 (advice line)

This organisation is open to all parents: natural or adoptive, with disability in the family, single parents, couples and stepfamilies, with children of all ages. Aims to prevent stress and breakdown in family life by providing advice line for parents, group counselling, and support projects for certain parents with specific needs.

Gingerbread
16–17 Clerkenwell Close
London EC1R OAA

0171 336 8183

Provides practical help and support for lone parents and their children via a nationwide network of over 250 self-help groups. Information given through individual groups; activities arranged for parents and children; some groups run day care schemes; back-up support available from the main London office.

National Council for One Parent Families
255 Kentish Town Road,
London NW5 2LX

0171 267 1361

Aims to improve the legal, economic and social position of one parent families. Runs an information service to lone parents and provides re-employment training for lone parents.

Family Welfare Association
501–505 Kingsland Road
London E8 4AU

0171 254 6251

Helps families and individuals to overcome the effects of poverty by providing emotional, practical and financial support. Runs family and children's centres and community mental health residential and day care.

Carers National Association
20–25 Glasshouse Yard
London ECIA 4JS

0171 490 8818
0171 490 8898 (carers line)

Helps anyone whose life is restricted because of caring for someone who is mentally or physically disabled or whose health is affected by old age or sickness. Information and advice service for carers; regular newsletter; puts carers in touch with one another.

ISSUE – The National Fertility Association
509 Aldridge Road
Great Barr
Birmingham B44 8NA

0121 344 4414

Provides help, information, representation and support to people with fertility difficulties. Factsheets, books and articles available as well as support from local contacts and ISSUE members. Telephone counselling available.

Gays

Lesbian Information Service
PO Box 8, Todmorden,
Lancs OL14 5TZ

01706 817235

Aims to raise the profile of lesbians generally and to publicise their needs. Generates positive activities to combat the oppression of lesbians. Exposes anti-lesbianism.

London Lesbian and Gay Switchboard
BM Switchboard
London WC1N 3XX
0171 837 7324

Provides a nationwide 24-hour telephone support service for lesbians and homosexual men; information such as topical data on all aspects of HIV/AIDS; counselling; referral service; contacts with social and befriending groups; sympathetic solicitors and health services around the country.

Addiction

Drinkline – The National Alcohol Helpline
Weddel House
7th Floor
13–14 West Smithfield
London EC1A 9DL

0171 332 0150
0345 320202 (helpline)

Helps and advises callers who are worried about their own

drinking; provides information on appropriate services and other forms of help; supports family and friends of those who are drinking.

Tranquilliser Anxiety Stress Help Association
60 High Street
Brentford
Middx TW8 0AH

0181 569 9933

Provides one-to-one counselling to those coming off tranquillisers, or suffering from stress and anxiety. Provides a helpline; group work; counselling and complementary therapy.

Narcotics Anonymous
UK Service Office
PO Box 1980
London N19 3LS

0171 272 9040
0171 730 0009 (helpline)

Offers help to anyone who wants to stop using drugs. Recovering drug addicts meet regularly to support each other to remain drug-free. Membership is open to all addicts regardless of the drug or combination of drugs used. This is a free service.

Turning Point
New Loom House
101 Back Church Lane
London E1 1LU

0171 702 2300

Offers residential rehabilitation, counselling and information to people with drug, alcohol-related and mental health problems. Support offered to families and friends of the drug or alcohol user. 45 projects nationwide. Other services include drop-in counselling services, telephone advice services and needle exchanges.

Debts

National Debtline
Birmingham Settlement
318 Summer Lane
Birmingham B19 3RL

0121 359 8501

Runs a free, independent and confidential telephone helpline to give advice to people in debt about their legal rights and options. They can issue callers with a self-help information pack.

Phobias

Phobics Society
4 Cheltenham Road
Chorlton-cum-Hardy
Manchester M21 9QN

0161 881 1937

Helps those suffering from anxiety disorders, such as phobias and obsessive/compulsive disorders. Self-help leaflets and contacts for sufferers available.

Eating disorders

Eating Disorders Association
Sackville Place
44 Magdalen Street
Norwich NR3 1JU

01603 621414

Offers support and mutual self-care to those suffering from anorexia and bulimia nervosa, and their families through a network of self-help groups, telephone helplines, information and newsletters.

Pre-Menstrual Syndrome

PMS Help
PO Box 160
St Albans
Herts AL1 4UQ

Helps sufferers of pre-menstrual syndrome, postnatal illness and other related hormonal illnesses, and their families. Provides printed information and videos.

Mental Health

MIND – National Association for Mental Health
Granta House
15–19 Broadway
Stratford
London E15 4BQ

0181 519 2122
0181 522 1728 (helpline)

Highlights the views and interests of people suffering from mental distress. Campaigns for good quality local mental health services. Headquarters London based, seven regional offices and 200 local associations. MIND nationally, regionally or locally (see your telephone directory for local associations) should be able to tell you of agencies and individuals offering different types of therapy or counselling though they cannot make recommendations:

Northern MIND
158 Durham Road
Gateshead NE8 4EL

0191 490 0109

North West MIND
21 Ribblesdale Place
Preston PR1 3NA

01772 821734

South East MIND
Kemp House
1st Floor
152–160 City Road
London EC1V 2NP

0171 608 0881

South West MIND
9th Floor
Tower House
Fair for Street
Bristol BS1 3BN

0117 925 0960

Trent and Yorkshire MIND
The White Building
Fitzalan Square
Sheffield S1 2AY

0114 272 1742

Wales MIND
23 St Mary Street
Cardiff CF1 2AA

01222 395123

West Midlands MIND
20–21 Cleveland Street
Wolverhampton WV1 3HT

01902 24404

Counselling and Therapy

Counselling

British Association for Counselling
1 Regent Place
Rugby
Warwicks CV21 2PJ

01788 550899

The BAC does not provide counselling direct but does provide information about counselling resources on a broad front. These include information sheets and directories, available from the above address.

Careline
Cardinal Heenan Centre
326 High Road
Ilford
Essex 1G1 1QP

0181 514 5444
0181 514 1177 (counselling)

Provides a confidential telephone counselling service for adults, young people and children on any issue, including child abuse, relationship problems, depression, loneliness, anxiety and phobias as well as HIV/AIDS related issues. Face-to-face counselling is also offered to adults. Information held on other agencies and support groups around the country.

The Isis Centre
43 Little Clarendon Street
Oxford OX1 2HS

01865 56648

An NHS counselling service for individuals, couples, families and groups. It is a self-referral service, and there is usually a waiting list before a first appointment. The secretary can be contacted by telephone for more detailed information.

Depressives Anonymous
36 Chestnut Avenue
Beverley
North Humberside HU17 9QU

01482 860619

Provides information on depression, and supports people suffering from, or who have suffered from, depression. Encourages the setting up of local groups around the UK.

London Rape Crisis Centre
PO Box 69
London WC1X 9NJ

0171 916 5466
0171 837 1600 (crisis line)

A confidential telephone helpline run by women for women and girls who have been raped or sexually assaulted at any time in their lives. This is a free service which is also open to relatives and friends for information and support.

Young People's Counselling Service
Tavistock Centre
120 Belsize Lane
London NW3 5BA

0171 435 7111 ext. 2337

Young people can contact this service direct for advice and counselling.

Divorce Mediation and Counselling Service
38 Ebury Street
London SW1W OLU

0171 730 2422

Provides a counselling and conciliation service to help parents who can no longer continue as partners to reach viable arrangements for joint care of their children without the need for going to court. To help individuals to talk about difficult situations that may arise in divorce or separation. Support also offered to childless couples and those with grown-up children.

Albany Trust
26 Balham Hill
London SW12 9EB

0181 675 6669

A personal counselling service for couples and individuals with all kinds of sexual identity and relationship problems.

BACUP (British Association of Cancer United Patients)
3 Bath Place
Rivington Street
London EC2A 3JR

0171 696 9000

Counselling at BACUP is free to anyone with cancer, and family members or friends who would like to talk to a counsellor. People are offered eight weekly sessions, of 50 minutes per session. Longer-term counselling may be possible. The service is confidential. For people living outside London, BACUP may be able to provide contacts for local counselling services.

Analysis

London Clinic of Psycho-Analysis
63 New Cavendish Street
London W1M 7RD

0171 436 1177

Offers five times a week psychoanalysis. Much of the work is done by trainees (as the clinic is attached to the major Institute, the British Psycho-Analytic Society) with careful supervision. Many of the analysts are medically qualified. Patients are assessed five times a week for, on average, two to three years. Fees are charged according to income. There is a Professional Practice Committee.

Association of Jungian Analysts
7 Eton Avenue,
London NW3 3EL

0171 794 8711

The clinic offers Jungian analysis with trainees under supervision and referrals can also be made with a member of AJA who is also a psychiatrist. Sessions are two or three times a week for at least a year, more likely two or longer. There is no NHS treatment. Fees for a clinic analysis are negotiated according to means, between £5 and £15. Fees with qualified analysts range from £25 to about £35. There are some members outside London, in Surrey, the West country, Kent and Cumbria.

C.G. Jung Clinic (The Society of Analytical Psychology)
1 Daleham Gardens
London NW3 5BY

0171 435 7696

Offers Jungian analysis. Much of the work is done by trainees, under careful supervision of experienced analysts. Patients are assessed first before a referral is made. Treatment is four times a week for a minimum period of two years. There is no NHS treatment and fees are not less than £6 per session. There is a Professional Practice Committee.

Psychotherapy

For NHS treatment contact your GP or call the Department of Psychology in the nearest general hospital. MIND (listed under Self-Help) is concerned that many areas seem to offer very little help of this kind, but MIND's regional offices (listed under Self Help) or local associations (look in the local telephone directory) may be able to help. Community Health Councils may also have information about local therapists.

British Association of Psychotherapists
37 Mapesbury Road
London NW2 4HJ

0181 452 9823

The BAP is concerned with the training of both adult and child analytical psychotherapists but it also offers a clinical assessment and referral service. This offers information and consultation to those who may be interested in having psychotherapy, and referral when appropriate. This assessment is with a professionally trained and experienced psychotherapist. Referral can then be made to either a trained member of BAP or a therapist in training. The orientation of BAP members is psychoanalytic, covering Freudian, Kleinian and Jungian views. Some are medically qualified. Treatment is one, two or three sessions a week and duration varies considerably. It cannot offer NHS treatment but the assessor for the clinical service may refer someone on to an NHS clinic if available. There is an Ethics Committee to deal with any complaints. The majority of the BAP's members are in London but it does have some in other areas such as Brighton, Bristol, Oxford and York. They will certainly try to refer someone within their area.

Tavistock Clinic
Adult Department
120 Belsize Lane
London NW3 5BA

0171 435 7111

The Tavistock Clinic is one of the country's leading institutions for training and research in psychotherapy. The Adult Department offers individual, group and marital psychotherapy, based on psychoanalytic principles. All patients referred to the Clinic are first offered an assessment during which a decision will be reached about whether psychoanalytic psychotherapy may be helpful. The average period of treatment is one to two years, although shorter-term therapy is also offered. Therapy is usually once a week but there is a limited number of more intensive therapy vacancies. All therapists are qualified psychiatrists, psychologists or social workers, and are either qualified psychoanalysts or adult psychotherapists or are undertaking specialist psychotherapy training. The Tavistock is an NHS unit and no fees are charged to patients.

Sex therapy

Help for a wide range of sexual problems is offered at all RELATE offices throughout the country (address of head office given in this section), but a growing number have specialised counsellors offering sex therapy. If your local office does not have such a specialist, they should be able to refer you to the nearest one that does. Professional referral is preferred but it is not essential. Fees are negotiable. There is always an initial assessment interview.

The following services, to be found in various parts of the country, also offer specialist sex therapy, often on the NHS:

Brook Advisory Centres

Family Planning Association Clinics

Some Departments of Psychiatry and Psychology in local general hospitals have sexual dysfunction clinics or psychosexual clinics.

The British Association for Counselling (address under Counselling) has a directory of agencies offering therapy, counselling and support for psychosexual problems.

The British Association for Sexual and Marital Therapy
PO Box 62
Sheffield S10 3TS

Provides information to the public about the local availability of sexual, marital and relationship therapy.

Institute of Psychosexual Medicine
11 Chandos Street
London WIM 9DE

0171 580 0631

Counselling available in psychosexual problems by doctors with specialist training in this area.

RELATE – National Marriage Guidance
Herbert Gray College
Little Church Street
Rugby, Warwicks CV21 3AP

01788 573241

RELATE has a network of around 130 centres nationwide which provide couple counselling for those with problems in relationships, psychosexual therapy, and relationship and family education.

Feminist therapy

Birmingham Women's Therapy Centre
The Lodge
53 Queensbridge Road
Moseley
Birmingham B13 8QD

0121 442 2241

Offers individual therapy and counselling. Therapists have a variety of orientations: psychoanalytic and humanistic but all basically feminist, seeing a woman's distress in terms of societal experience. There is always an initial assessment. Treatment is free. All the workers are qualified as social workers and/or counsellors.

Women's Counselling and Therapy Service
Oxford Chambers
Oxford Place
Leeds LS1 3AX

0113 245 5725

WCTS offers psychodynamic psychotherapy from a feminist perspective. Initial consultations are with a senior therapist. Individual therapy, analytic and topic based groups. Expertise in working with sexual abuse, eating disorders and differences of race, culture and sexuality. No fees are charged but clients are encouraged to make a donation according to their means.

The Women's Therapy Centre
6 Manor Gardens
London N7 6LA

0171 263 6200

Offers individual long-term and short-term therapy, analytically orientated, and group therapy. All the therapists have a professional training and the majority have a psychodynamic orientation – Freudian, objects relations, Kleinian, Jungian. New clients are always given an initial interview with a therapist to see whether the therapy is appropriate and whether the client and therapist think they can work together. Because of very limited resources, the Centre also has a referral network of therapists in London and other parts of the country. Individual therapy is once a week, and groups also meet once a week. The time contract is agreed between therapist and client at the outset, and can either be open-ended or limited to one or two years. Fees are on a sliding scale, according to the client's income and circumstances. The therapists treat people with a wide range of problems but the Centre has developed a particular approach to working with women who have eating disorders. The Centre may be able to refer clients to feminist therapists in other parts of the country.

Individual therapy

Nafsiyat
278 Seven Sisters Road
London N4 2HY

0171 263 4130

Psychodynamic techniques are used by the therapists and counsellors who come from a range of ethnic and cultural backgrounds. Special account is taken of the cultural factors and contextual differences involved. Patients are assessed before referral to therapists at the Centre. Treatment may last two weeks, a few months or over a year, according to the patient's needs. Therapists see children, adolescents, adults, couples, families and groups. Some patients are seen in their own home. The psychotherapy is free to patients living within the Camden and Islington health district. A fee of around £15 is charged to those people coming from other areas. There is a professional committee which deals with complaints.

For more information on individual psychotherapy outside London contact: British Association of Psychotherapists (listed under Psychotherapy).

Wellbeing

Institute for Complementary Medicine
PO Box 194
London SE16 1QZ

0171 237 5165

Aims to reduce suffering and increase the quality of patients' health by ensuring the best possible natural treatments are made available to them on the same terms as other types of medicine. Supplies information to the public and develops new methods of natural health care.

British Homeopathic Association
27a Devonshire Street
London W1N 1RJ

0171 935 2163

Aims to spread the knowledge and use of 'First Aid' homeopathy among members of the public; promotes homeopathic treatment inside and outside the National Health Service; maintains a specialist lending library; holds contacts for doctors practising homeopathy.

British Holistic Medical Association
R. T. Trust
Rowland Thomas House
Royal Shrewsbury Hospital South
Mytton Oak Road
Shrewsbury
Shropshire SY3 8XF

Promotes an awareness of the holistic approach to health; fostering a balance between body, mind and spirit; promotes education concerning health rather than just treatment of disease; runs courses and seminars to encourage self-healing; supplies self-help tapes; supports a wide range of orthodox and complementary methods of intervention, aims to develop a sense of partnership between doctors and patients.

Keep Fit Association
Francis House
Francis Street
London SW1P 1DE

0171 233 8898

Provides the opportunity for women of all ages and aptitudes to develop their potential by making full use of their physical and intellectual capabilities through the medium of movement.

Relaxation for Living
29 Burwood Park Road
Walton on Thames
Surrey KT12 5LH

Teaches people in small classes and by correspondence; promotes stress management through physical relaxation and aims to improve health.

Women's Nutritional Advisory Service
PO Box 268
Lewes
East Sussex BN7 2JA

01273 487366
0839 556615 (helpline)

Provides nutritional information and research for women suffering from the menopause and PMT; runs clinics and monitors individual nutritional programmes by post (for a fee).

Hysterectomy Support Network
3 Lynne Close
Green Street Green
Orpington
Kent BR6 6BS

Provides information and support for women and their partners; support offered by letter or telephone by women who have had a hysterectomy themselves; encourages self-help and the setting up of support groups.

Breast Cancer Care
210 New Kings Road
London SW6 4NZ

0171 384 2344 (helpline)
0500 245345 (free helpline)

Aims to relieve the anxiety and help in the recovery of women who have breast cancer or other breast disorders. Offers advice and assistance; counselling; information and comfort including emotional support from volunteers who have had breast cancer. Free leaflets available; helplines; a prosthesis fitting service.

Amarant Trust
11–13 Charter House Buildings
London EC1M 7AN

0171 490 1644
0891 660620/660630 (24-hour helplines – premium rate numbers)

Promotes a better understanding of the menopause and hormone replacement therapy. Aims to make treatment available to the women who need it. Runs menopause counselling and hormone replacement therapy clinics; setting up voluntary self-help groups throughout the country.

National Osteoporosis Society
PO Box 10
Radstock
Bath
Avon BA3 3YB

01761 432472

Aims to relieve sickness and advance medical knowledge in relation to osteoporosis and related conditions. Helps sufferers by letter, telephone, newsletters, publications and by the setting up of groups.

Refuge
PO Box 855
London W4 4JF

0181 747 0133
0181 995 4430 (24-hour crisis line)

Provides temporary/emergency accommodation for women and children escaping from domestic violence as well as counselling, information and follow-up support.

Age-Link
Suite 9/10
The Manor House
The Green
Southall
Middx UB2 4BJ

0181 571 5888

Elderly, isolated, housebound people can use Age-Link

as a community resource. It aims to establish groups of volunteers, mostly young people, who will take out and befriend people who have little chance to leave their homes without help.